LONGMAN BUSINESS ENGLISH S

Giving presentations

MARK ELLIS AND NINA O'DRISCOLL

Longman

SERIES EDITOR NINA O'DRISCOLL
WITH MARK ELLIS AND ADRIAN PILBEAM

The authors work for Language Training Services

Longman Group UK Limited,
Longman House, Burnt Mill, Harlow,
Essex CM20 2JE, England
and Associated Companies throughout the world.

First published 1992

Designed and set by Design Locker in
Monotype PostScript Gill Sans 10 on 12pt

Produced by Longman Group (FE) Ltd

Printed in Hong Kong

ISBN 0582 06441 4

Acknowledgements

We are grateful to the following for their permission to reproduce
copyright material: The Economist/The World In 1991 for pages 61
(top) and 64. Readers Digest Association/Eurodata for page 65 (top).

Cartoons by Pat Drennan and Noel Ford
Cover photograph by Tony Stone Worldwide

Contents

Unit 4: Referring to visuals

Unit 5: Concluding the presentation

Unit 6: Handling questions

Introduction to the learner

Giving Presentations is part of the *Longman Business English Skills* series. It will improve your skills in giving presentations in business and other professional situations.

Objectives

The material can be used by people who already have a good level of English and need to give presentations in work-related situations.

The material will improve your skills in giving presentations by helping you to:

- organise your points so that your audience will find it easy to follow your argumentation
- deliver your presentation in an interesting and engaging way
- keep your audience listening
- answer your audience's questions

The material

You can use the material on your own, or with a teacher. It consists of an audio-cassette and a book. The book and the cassette should be used together.

The cassette contains all the model presentations and practice material.

All the material on the cassette is marked 📼 in the book.

There are six units. Each unit covers a different aspect of a presentation, ranging from developing an introduction, organising the information, developing a conclusion to handling questions from the audience.

The focus of the material is primarily on the **verbal** aspects of giving a presentation. It does not attempt to deal with the non-verbal aspects of a presentation e.g. eye contact and gestures or other body language.

Each of the six units has the following main sections.

A Preparation

This section introduces an aspect of giving a presentation or introduces the context for the main presentation in the unit.

B What to say

This part of the unit contains useful language for different stages of a presentation e.g. the unit on introductions focusses on different ways to express the purpose of a presentation, while the unit on the persuasive presentation focusses on how to build up arguments to support a position.

C How to organise the information

This section of each unit deals with aspects of organisation ranging from language that will make the structure of a presentation clear to ways of reinforcing key points.

D How to create interest

This looks at some of the techniques you can use to engage and maintain your audience's interest through the presentation. It also looks at aspects of delivery, the way you sound when you are giving a presentation. This step is marked ▶))) in the book.

E Activities

This contains one or two presentation tasks to practise all the points covered in the unit.

There is no key to these activities. If you are working on your own, we recommend you record yourself either on audio-cassette or video. This step is marked 🔍(((. When you play back your presentation you can use the checklist to help you assess the progress you are making.

Sections B, C and D have the following steps:

Focus

This is a listening stage which involves listening to extracts from a presentation. While you are listening you fill in the missing words. You may need to stop the cassette and play some extracts several times. The purpose of this step is to present language which will be useful to you in the practice tasks, and also when you have to give your own presentations.

Summary

This gives you a summary of useful language and presentation techniques. You should refer to this before you do the practice tasks for the section. You may find it helpful as reference material when you are planning your own presentations.

Tasks

This is a series of tasks to practise the language and points from this section of the unit. Some of these tasks are on cassette.

The key

After each unit there is a key. This contains the tapescripts for all the recorded materials in the unit and model versions for the tasks in the different parts of the unit.

Remember that the answers in the *Tasks* sections in each unit are only suggested answers. If your version is different, it will not be wrong as long as it has a similar style and form to the suggested answers.

Introductions

A Preparation

When giving a presentation it is essential to have a clear idea of what you want to achieve e.g. Do you want to *inform* your audience about essential facts, or to *persuade* them to accept your proposal? This main purpose or aim needs to be briefly stated in the opening part of a presentation.

 1. Listen to tape A1. You will hear the introductions from four presentations.
Complete the statements below.
a. In presentation one the presenter wants the audience to accept ....
b. In presentation two the presenter wants to inform the audience about ....
c. In presentation three the presenter wants to explain ....
d. In presentation four the presenter wants to convince his audience to ....

Check your answers in the key **A1**

There are many different techniques you can use to begin a presentation.

One common technique is to state the objectives and the main points which you will include in the presentation. But if you want to catch your audience's attention more quickly, there are other techniques e.g. you can relate the subject to the real-life experience of your audience, or use some surprising facts.

2. Identify the main technique (a–d below) the presenter uses in each of the four introductions you have just heard.

If necessary, listen to each introduction again.
In which introduction does the presenter:
a. Use surprising and relevant facts to gain the audience's attention?
b. Simply state the objectives and outline the points to be developed?
c. Involve the audience by getting them to do something?
d. Use a true event to help illustrate the purpose?

Check your answers in the key   A2

B What to say – Stating the purpose

B1 Focus

A good introduction should include a brief statement explaining the purpose of the presentation.

Listen to tape B1. You will hear extracts from the four introductions.
This time pick out the phrases which the presenters use to state the purpose of their presentations.

Introduction 1

Context An internal company meeting, at which a consultant presents the results of a study.
Audience Key managers from different European subsidiaries.

What .... this morning
.... the results of our study into the consolidation of your computer activities in Europe ...

Introduction 2

Context An international medical conference.
Audience Other delegates, medical doctors and scientific researchers.

No, it's not the famous store! In this case the letters stand for chocolate addiction, which ....
.... presentation ...

Introduction 3

Context   An international engineering conference.
Audience   Other delegates, mainly engineering specialists.

… consequences. .... , ...
.... today .... the
technical problems involved in lighting tunnels, and .... the
investments we intend to make to improve efficiency and safety.

Introduction 4

Context   An internal company meeting about training for plant operators.
Audience   Representatives from training and personnel at the company's different
locations around the world.

… the procedures. .... , ... this
morning .... two new techniques which
we need to incorporate in our CBT packages to improve our operator training.

Check your answers in the key   **B1**

B2 Summary

Stating the purpose

- In your introduction state the purpose of your presentation
  - why are you there?
  - what are you going to talk about?

  You can do this
  - right at the beginning.
  - by building up gradually, leaving your statement of purpose until the latter part of the introduction.

  Both ways can be equally effective.

- Here are some useful expressions for stating the purpose of the presentation.

  In my presentation I'll be proposing two new techniques which we need to incorporate in our CBT packages to improve our operator training.

  In my presentation today I'm going to explain the technical problems involved in lighting tunnels.

  This morning I'd like to review progress on the AFTA project.

  The subject/topic of this presentation is CBT for operator training.

- If you want to create more impact, you can change the normal word order and begin your statement of purpose with the word 'what' e.g.

  What I'd like to do this morning is present the results of our study.

  What I'm going to explain this afternoon are the technical problems involved in lighting tunnels.

  What I'll be proposing in my presentation are two new techniques which we need to incorporate in our CBT packages to improve our operator training.

B3 Tasks

I. Listen to tape B3.1. You will hear the last three statements in the summary. Notice how the presenters create impact by stressing words and by pausing. As you listen, mark where the presenters pause. Follow the example. The pause is marked ☐.

Example

What I'd like to do this morning ☐ is to present the results of our study.

a. What I'm going to explain this afternoon are the technical problems involved in lighting tunnels.

b. What I'll be proposing in my presentation are two new techniques which we need to incorporate in our CBT packages to improve our operator training.

Check your answers in the key **B3.1**

2. Look at the table below.

What would you say to outline the purpose of the three presentations? Complete the phrases on the right. The first one has been done for you as an example.

Purpose	Your words
Analyse the market for luxury holidays in the US.	In this presentation *I'll be analysing the market for luxury holidays in the US.*
a. Review the performance of Aqua-Sparkle.	In my presentation today I'd like to ....
b. Examine the case for a new blend of coffee for the French market.	This morning I'm going to ....

Check your answers in the key **B3.2**

3. Now restate the purpose of the presentations in B3.1, but give them more impact by beginning each statement with *what*. Follow the example.

Example

What I'll be analysing in this presentation is the market for luxury holidays in the US.
or
What I'll be doing in this presentation is to analyse the market for luxury holidays in the US.

Now listen to the model versions on tape B3.3.

C How to organise the information – Outlining the development

CI Focus

Many successful introductions include information about the *main points* to be developed during the presentation, and the *order* in which the presenter will develop these. This is called *signposting*.

Listen to tape C1.

You will hear the first introduction again. Notice how the presenter explains the main points she will develop later in the presentation. As you listen complete the missing words in the extract. Then read the notes on the right.

Introduction 1: The consolidation of European computing at Marcon Chemicals

Extract	Notes

What I'd like to do this morning is to present the results of our study into the consolidation of your computer activities in Europe.

States the purpose of the presentation

....

Outlines three main points to be developed

three .... points .

.... , ... some background information about the LX project team ...

First point

.... , ... outlining the objectives of the team,

Second point

.... the current organisation of your European data centres.

.... , ... our recommendations ...

Third point

Check your answers in the key   `C1`

C2 Summary

Signposting a presentation

- Your introduction should contain some kind of signposting for the audience.
  - tell them what you will be talking about.
  - tell them in which order you will develop your points.

- Signposting your presentation will help you:
  - to define the limits of the presentation.
  - to focus the audience on the aspects of the topic you want to talk about.

- Here are some useful expressions for signposting a presentation.

  I'll be developing three main points.

  First, I'll give you ... Second, ... Lastly, ...

  My presentation will be in two main parts. In the first part I'll ... And then I'll ...

  Firstly, I'd like to ... Secondly, we can ... And I'll finish with ...

C3 Tasks

1. Expand the three introductions in B3.2.

The introduction should include
- your statement of purpose.
- information about the main points which you will develop.

The first one has been done for you as an example.

Purpose	Main points
Analyse the market for luxury holidays in the US.	1. Holiday trends over last two years in the US. 2. My ideas for types of holidays to offer.

Example

In this presentation I'll be analysing the market for luxury holidays in the US. In the first part of the presentation I'll be looking at holiday trends over the last two years in the US. Then, I'll give you my ideas about the type of holidays we should be offering.

a. Review the performance of Aqua-Sparkle.	1. Overview of fizzy drinks market. 2. Performance of Aqua-Sparkle. 3. Outlook for the next two years.
b. Examine the case for a new blend of coffee for the French market.	1. General background about types of coffee. 2. Patterns in coffee consumption in France. 3. Our proposal for a new blend.

Check your answers in the key C3.1

2. Listen to tape C3.2. You will hear *Introduction one* again. Notice how the presenter highlights the structure of her presentation by stressing these words *first, then* and *lastly*.

Notice also that there is a pause ☐ after each of them.

Introduction 1 – The consolidation of the data centres

<u>First</u> ☐ I'll give you some background information about the LX project team ...

<u>Then</u> ☐ after outlining the objectives of the team, I'll go on to examine the current organisation of your European data centres.

<u>Lastly</u> ☐ I'll explain our recommendations for maximising the efficiency of those centres.

3. Listen to tape C3.3. You will hear *Introduction two* again.

Notice how the presenter highlights the structure of his presentation.
Mark the three places where the presenter pauses and the words he stresses to highlight the structure.

Introduction 2 – Chocolate addiction

My first point will be to define what chocolate addiction is ...

Then I'll give you some clinical data about chocolate addiction ...

And finally I'll describe the treatment suitable for acute forms of addiction ...

Check your answers in the key C3.3

4. You are at an international conference on Human Resources. You are going to give a presentation to other delegates about selection and orientation procedures for employees due to go abroad.

Develop the notes below as an introduction for your presentation.

Include:
- A statement of purpose.
- Signposting to outline the main points which you will develop in the presentation.

Background	Increasing globalisation of business – essential to select right people for overseas assignments.
Purpose	Look at the factors involved when identifying personnel to work abroad.
Points to develop	1. Costs of sending people abroad. 2. Reasons why so many people return home before the end of their contracts. 3. Characteristics of good assignee. 4. Selection and orientation procedures.

If possible record yourself when you give the introduction.

Pay attention to the use of pauses and stress when you explain how you will develop the presentation.

Now listen to a model version for the presentation on tape C3.4.

D How to create interest – Involving your audience

When giving a presentation it is, of course, very important to engage the attention of the audience right at the beginning of the presentation. One way to do this is to make your introduction as interesting and lively as possible.

D1 Focus

Listen to tape D1. You will hear *Introduction three* again.

Introduction 3 – Improved lighting in tunnels

1. Notice how the presenter starts this highly technical presentation with some unusual statistics about tunnels. He includes these to engage his audience's attention.

The four facts are listed on page 14. Complete the sentences he uses to present these facts to his audience.

1. **Fact**   One of the noticeable features of the *Autostrada del Sole* is the number of tunnels ...

   His words   And no doubt, ... have driven along the

   famous *Autostrada del Sole*, ... the large number of tunnels ...

   Notice how he refers to the personal experience of the audience to illustrate this point.

2. **Fact**   There are approximately 300 kms of tunnels in Italy.

   His words   In fact, here in Italy, ... about 300 kms of tunnels.

   Notice how he personalises the information by using *we have* rather than *there are*.

3. **Fact**   Energy consumption for lighting tunnels is very high.

   His words   .... , for example, that the total energy

   consumption for lighting this network of tunnels .... to

   lighting .... of Turin?

   Notice how he does not give actual energy consumption figures, but paints a picture which the audience can relate to.

4. **Fact**   80 per cent of accidents in tunnels are caused by bad lighting.

   His words   In fact, ... accidents in tunnels can be attributed to bad lighting.

   Notice how he does not give the percentage, but makes the figures easier for the audience to relate to.

Check your answers in the key   **DI**

D2 Summary

Involving the audience

- While doing research for your presentation, you may discover unusual or interesting facts and statistics about the topic. Include some of them in your introduction.
- Present them in a way that makes it easy for the audience to relate to them.
  e.g. *One person in four* may be easier to relate to than '25 per cent of the population'.
- Use words like *you, your, us, our* to make your audience feel involved in your presentation.
- Illustrate the point of your presentation with examples or stories from life. This will help to bring your presentation to life.
- Ask the audience to do something e.g. ask for a show of hands.
- Ask the audience questions to involve them in the presentation. This is particularly appropriate for informal presentations when you have a small audience.
- With larger audiences use rhetorical questions – questions which encourage the audience to think, but which you answer yourself.

(See unit 2 for more about rhetorical questions)

D3 Tasks

1. Present these facts in a way that will involve the audience and make the facts easier to relate to.

Follow the example.

More than 25 per cent of European flights are delayed by more than 30 minutes.

Next time **you** take a flight in Europe, at least **one in four** of **you** can expect delays of well over 30 minutes.

  a. More than 60 per cent of executives suffer from major stress during their careers.

  b. A person spends approximately 2,600 hours asleep each year, which is a considerable part of their lives.

Check your answers in the key   D3.1

2. You are the export manager of a British manufacturer of prestigious sports cars.

Your company wants to increase its exports. At the moment exports represent 30 per cent of the business and are mainly to the US. The problem is there are signs that the US market for sports cars is slowing down.

You have been asked to prepare a presentation for the meeting outlined below.

Context A company meeting to discuss marketing strategy.

Audience The management of the company.

Purpose To present Japan as an attractive new market for your range of sports cars.

Prepare an introduction for the presentation.
Start with some relevant background and end by stating the purpose of the presentation.

Include these surprising facts as evidence that your cars will sell well in Japan.
- A *BMW* is on display at Tokyo's Narita Airport.
- Left-hand drive *Mercedes* are bought even though the Japanese drive on the left.

Check your answers in the key   D3.2

3. Listen to tape D3.3. You will hear *Introduction four* again. In this introduction the presenter involves his audience by:

  a. Using a real-life event to illustrate the point of his presentation.

  b. Creating a personal and informal style.

As you listen, complete the words he uses to state these ideas.

Introduction 4 – New techniques for computer-based training

1. **Idea** For some years computer-based training has been used to train operators to carry out plant operations.

His words .... , for some years now, ...

.... CBT, computer-based training, to train operators in our power stations to carry out different plant operations.

2. **Idea**   The Chernobyl accident demonstrates that training, which only trains operators to carry out a set of operations, is inadequate.

   His words   The experience of Chernobyl has shown .... that ....

   .... to train an operator to carry out a certain set of operations.

3. **Idea**   The operator needs training which provides an understanding of the process behind the procedures.

   His words   ... in other words .... training needs to provide the operator with an understanding of the process behind the procedures.

   Check your answers in the key   D3.3

4. The script below is the introduction for a presentation about sleep patterns and how they relate to executive stress.

   Re-work the introduction to:

   a. Make the style more personal.

   b. Give the content more impact for the audience.

   > ## Script
   >
   > Most people spend approximately 2,600 hours per year asleep. The purpose of this presentation is to present the findings of a study into people's sleep habits. The study suggests that the time an individual spends asleep is inversely related to salary – companies which offer high salaries encourage individuals to substitute work for sleep.
   >
   > The presentation is divided in two parts. The first part describes the findings of the study in more detail. The second part examines the implications for executive stress.

   Check your answers in the key   D3.4

E Activities

1. Choose one of the subjects below for a presentation.

   ~ *Water*   ~ *Transportation in my city*   ~ *Traffic*   ~ *Energy sources in my country*
   ~ *The environment*   ~ *Air travel*   ~ *The press*   ~ *Pollution in towns*   ~ *Stress in life*

   a. Complete the details about the presentation you are planning.

   Context
   Audience
   Purpose

b. Brainstorm some points which you can develop in the presentation.

c. Decide on your main points and an appropriate order in which to present them.

d. Prepare an introduction for the presentation. Do it in two ways:
   i. Include a statement of purpose and a clear plan of the points you will develop.
   ii Bring your introduction to life.

Include questions, unusual or interesting facts or illustrate it with real life events.

2. Prepare an introduction for your own presentation.

Use one of the frameworks below to help you organise your ideas.

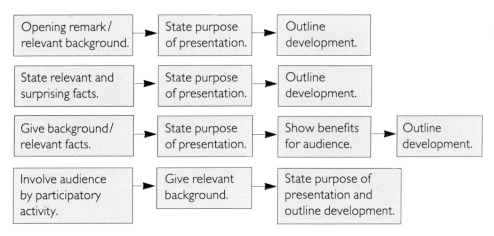

If possible record yourself. When you play back your introduction, use the checklist below to help you evaluate your presentation.

CHECKLIST

	Yes/No	Example phrases

■ Did you explain to the audience:
  – Who you are?
  – Why you are speaking?

■ Did you include a statement of purpose?

■ Did you include signposting?

■ Did you relate the presentation to the needs of the audience?

■ How did you involve the audience?

■ Did your opening remarks include:
  – a participatory activity?
  – a question to the audience?
  – surprising / unusual facts?

Answer key

A Preparation

AI

a. the recommendations of the study.

b. treatments for chocolate addiction.

c. future investments to improve the lighting in tunnels in Italy.

d. improve their computer based training for plant operators by incorporating two new techniques.

A2

a. Introduction 3

b. Introduction I

c. Introduction 2

d. Introduction 4

AI 🔲

Introduction I

PRESENTER: Good morning. My name is Sarah Benson and, as you know, I work as a consultant for the LX Consulting Group. You've all been aware of the presence of myself and two of my colleagues over the past couple of weeks, and I'd like to thank you very much for your cooperation and understanding.

What **I'd like to do** this morning **is to present** the results of our study into the consolidation of your computer activities in Europe. I'm going to be developing three main points. First, I'll give you some background information about the LX project team which, as many of you will know, was set up three months ago to study levels of computer activity. Then, after outlining the objectives of the team, I'll go on to examine the current organisation of your European data centres. Lastly, I'll explain our recommendations for maximising the efficiency of those centres.

Introduction 2

MASTER OF CEREMONIES: Good morning, ladies and gentlemen. It's my privilege today to introduce Dr Martin Roberts who is going to be talking to us about addiction. His specific area of interest

is rather unusual, so perhaps I'd better let him introduce the subject in detail. Dr Roberts.

PRESENTER: Good morning. Before I get down to the serious business of the presentation, I'd just like you to think for a few seconds what these letters, C and A, stand for …

No, it's not the famous store! In this case the letters stand for chocolate addiction, which **is the subject of my** presentation. My first point will be to define what chocolate addiction is – in the scientific sense, that is. Then, I'll give you some clinical data about chocolate addiction – this, I'm sure, will be of particular interest to those of you involved in the area of hyperactive children. And finally, I'll describe the treatment suitable for acute forms of addiction.

Introduction 3

PRESENTER: I imagine many of you here today have been to Italy on holiday. And no doubt, some of you have driven along the famous *Autostrada del Sole*, and noticed the large number of tunnels which have been carved through the rock. In fact, here in Italy, we have about 300 km of tunnels. But, what about the lighting of these? Did you know, for example, that the total energy consumption for lighting this network of tunnels is equivalent to lighting a city the size of Turin?

But, in spite of all this investment, much of the lighting is inadequate, and is the cause of many car accidents.

In fact, eight out of ten accidents in tunnels can be attributed to bad lighting, and many of these have fatal consequences. **So, in my presentation** today **I'm going to explain** the technical problems involved in lighting tunnels, and **outline** the investments we intend to make to improve efficiency and safety.

Introduction 4

PRESENTER: As you know, for some years now, we've been using CBT, computer based training to train operators in our power stations to carry out different plant operations. However, the experience of Chernobyl has shown us that it is not enough simply to train an operator to carry out a certain set of operations, to know which switch to push or which button to press. He or she must also be aware of the effect of these actions on the whole process of the plant – in other words our training needs to provide the operator with an understanding of the process behind the procedures. **So, in my presentation** this morning **I'll be proposing** two new techniques which we need to incorporate in our CBT packages to improve our operator training.

B *What to say*

B1

See tapescript A1 above. The missing words are in **bold**.

B3.1 📼

(Example)
What I'd like to do this morning ☐ is to present the results of our study.
a. What I'm going to explain this afternoon ☐ are the technical problems involved in lighting tunnels.
b. What I'll be proposing in my presentation ☐ are two new techniques ☐ which we need to incorporate into our CBT packages ☐ to improve our operator training.

B3.2

a. In my presentation today I'd like to review the performance of Aqua-Sparkle.
b. This morning I'm going to examine the case for a new blend of coffee for the French market.

B3.3 📼 **Model versions**

(Example)
What I'll be analysing in this presentation is the market for luxury holidays in the US.
or
What I'll be doing in this presentation is to analyse the market for luxury holidays in the US.
a. What I'd like to do in my presentation today is review the performance of Aqua-Sparkle.
or

What I'd like to review in my presentation today is the performance of Aqua-Sparkle.
b. What I'm going to do this morning is examine the case for a new blend of coffee for the French market.
or
What I'm going to examine this morning is the case for a new blend of coffee for the French market.

C *How to organise the information.*

C1

**I'm going to be developing … main
First, I'll give you
Then, after … I'll go on to examine
Lastly, I'll explain**

C1 📼

Refer to tape A1 (introduction 1) for the full tapescript.

C3.1 Model version

a. In my presentation today I'd like to review the performance of Aqua-Sparkle. The presentation will be in three main parts. First, I'll present an overview of the fizzy drinks market. Second, we can look at the performance of Aqua-Sparkle. And finally, I'd like to give you the outlook for the next two years.
b. This morning I'm going to examine the case for a new blend of coffee for the French market. I'll begin with some background about different types of coffee Then, we can go on and look at patterns of coffee consumption in France. Lastly, I'll explain why I think the French market needs a new blend.

C3.2 📼

Refer to tape A1 (Introduction 1) for the full tapescript.

C3.3

My <u>first</u> point ☐ will be to define what chocolate addiction is …

<u>Then</u> ☐ I'll give you some clinical data about chocolate addiction …

And <u>finally</u> ☐ I'll describe …

C3.3 📼

Refer to tape A1 (introduction 2) for the full tapescript.

C3.4 📼 Model version

PRESENTER: With the increasing globalisation of business, it's essential to select the right people for overseas assignments. And in this presentation, I'd like to look at the factors involved when identifying personnel to work abroad.

I'll be looking at four points. First, the costs of sending our people abroad. Second, the reasons why so many people return home before the end of their contracts. Third, the characteristics of a good assignee. And finally, I'll spend some time talking about the selection and orientation procedures we've developed to deal with this task.

D How to create interest

DI
1. ... **some of you** ... **and noticed** ...
2. **we have** ...
3. **Did you know** ... **is equivalent** ... **a city the size** ...
4. ... **eight out of ten** ...

DI 📼
Refer to tape AI (introduction 3) for the full tapescript.

D3.I Model version
a. Did you know that six out of ten executives in our company can expect to suffer from stress during their working lives?
b. Each of you will spend around a third of your life sleeping, which is, when you think about it, a significant part of your life.

D3.2 Model version
PRESENTER: On a recent visit to Japan, I was greatly surprised to see a German car, a *BMW*, prominently displayed in Tokyo's main airport. I was even more surprised to see so many left-hand drive *Mercedes* in Tokyo itself, especially as the Japanese today drive on the left. Clearly, there's a lucrative market for quality foreign cars. So I will be presenting Japan as a new and attractive market for our range of prestigious sports cars, and as the solution to the downturn in our US business.

D3.3
1. **As you know ... we've been using** ...
2. ... **us** ... **it is not enough simply** ...
3. ... **our** ...

D3.3 📼
Refer to tape AI (introduction 4) for the full tapescript.

D3.4 Model version
This morning I'd like to present the findings of a study into people's sleep habits. I'm sure this will be of great interest to everyone here, especially when you consider that each of us will spend about a third of our life sleeping.

In fact, this study suggests that the amount of time an individual spends asleep is inversely related to salary. In other words, by offering employees more money we encourage them to substitute work for sleep.

In the first part of my presentation we'll be looking at these surprising findings in more detail. Then, we can discuss the implications for executive stress.

The informative presentation

A Preparation

The main purpose of many business and technical presentations is to give the audience information or facts, for example, about the performance of a particular product.

The visuals below are from an informative presentation given at an international sales meeting of the Marwell Food Group.

Look through the two OHP transparencies and complete the statements on the right.

CONSUMER PURCHASES IN THE UK			
TOTAL FIZZY DRINK MARKET	-3%		
TOTAL LEMONADE MARKET	-7%		
AQUA-SPARKLE			
North	-1%	Midlands	-7%
South	-14%	Scotland	-6%

1. The overall performance of the lemonade category was

   . . . .

2. The best performance was in

   . . . .

3. Consumer purchases were seven per cent

   . . . .

   last year's figures across the country.

YEAR TO DATE SALES PERFORMANCE OF AQUA-SPARKLE					

6 MONTHS' SALES

LITRES 000	YTD	LYTD	VAR	PLAN	VAR VS PLAN
National Grocers	24500	23500	+4%	24500	0%
Independent Grocers	3250	3750	-13%	3800	-14%
Neighbourhood Stores	9500	9700	-2%	10000	-5%

Key: YTD = Year to date   LYTD = Last year to date   VAR = Variance

4. The most solid performance was in the

....

sector.

5. The Independent Grocers sector was

....

per cent down on last year.

Check your answers in the key **A**

B What to say – Describing and analysing performance

B1 Focus

Listen to tape B1.

You will hear four extracts from the presentation in which the UK Sales Manager analyses the performance of Aqua-Sparkle over the last six months.

As you listen, complete the missing words in each extract. Then read the notes on the right.

Extract 1

A key area of concern is the southern region where

purchases .... 14 per cent.

....

.... decline .... reduced disposable income

in this area .... very high interest

rates, ... high
commitments on mortgages and other types of loans.

Notes

Describes the trend

Gives explanation

Expands explanation

Extract 2

First, the National Grocers. This sector ....   *Describes the trend*

.... the ....

with a .... last year.

A ....   *Gives explanation*

.... the one-pack promotional campaign within   *Adds comment*
National Grocers, which is clearly having the desired effect
on sales.

Extract 3

In the second sector, Independent Grocers, the brand
          Describes the trend
.... As you can see, the rate of sales   *and comments on it*

.... last
year, and several customers have actually delisted
Aqua-Sparkle, which is obviously a very worrying trend.

.... here ....   *Gives explanation*
price. Competitors have been discounting heavily with a

.... in retail shelf-price. This means   *Expands explanation*
that now, in this sector, Aqua-Sparkle is priced much higher
than the competition.

Extract 4

... gross profit ....   *Describes the trend*

.... with the profit per litre up 2.7p on last year.

.... two .... for ....

.... , a better control of discounts.   *Gives first explanation*
As I said, we're deliberately not discounting in order to   *Expands explanation*
maintain the premium positioning of the brand.

.... , we've managed to achieve a reduction in   *Gives second*
packaging costs.   *explanation*

Check your answers in the key ▐ B1

B2 Summary

Describing performance to date

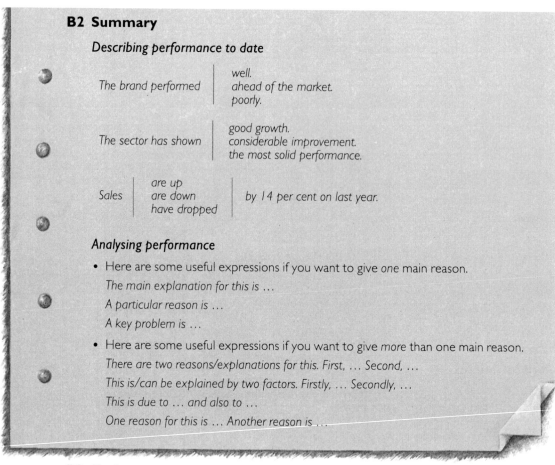

The brand performed	well.
	ahead of the market.
	poorly.

The sector has shown	good growth.
	considerable improvement.
	the most solid performance.

Sales	are up	
	are down	by 14 per cent on last year.
	have dropped	

Analysing performance

* Here are some useful expressions if you want to give *one* main reason.

  The main explanation for this is …

  A particular reason is …

  A key problem is …

* Here are some useful expressions if you want to give *more* than one main reason.

  There are two reasons/explanations for this. First, … Second, …

  This is/can be explained by two factors. Firstly, … Secondly, …

  This is due to … and also to …

  One reason for this is … Another reason is …

B3 Tasks

1. The OHP transparency below is from a presentation reviewing the performance of anti-ageing creams.

Study the information on the OHP transparency.

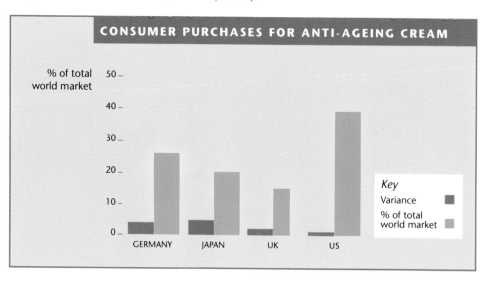

CONSUMER PURCHASES FOR ANTI-AGEING CREAM

Key:
Variance
% of total world market

What would you say to describe the performance of anti-ageing creams in the markets below?

Follow the example.

Market	Performance
Germany	Good growth, sales up ten per cent

The German market has shown good growth with sales up by ten per cent on last year.
or
The German market has shown good growth with a ten per cent increase in sales.

a. Japan	Ahead of the market
b. UK	Disappointing, four per cent increase
c. US	Poorly, slight increase of two per cent

Check your answers in the key B3.1

2. The notes below summarise three main points for a presentation reviewing the performance of chocolate products.

What would you say to develop each point?

Follow the example.

Point 1

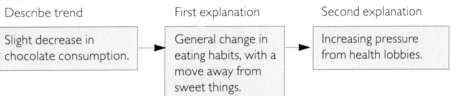

Describe trend	First explanation	Second explanation
Slight decrease in chocolate consumption.	General change in eating habits, with a move away from sweet things.	Increasing pressure from health lobbies.

There's been a slight decrease in chocolate consumption. One reason for this is a general change in eating habits, with a move away from sweet things. Another reason is increasing pressure from health lobbies.

Point 2

Describe trend	First explanation	Expand explanation
Market for boxes of chocolates always difficult.	Seasonal market.	Major sales around Christmas – lower sales volume for the rest of the year.

Point 3

Describe trend	Add comment	First explanation
Sales of bags of chocolates well below target.	Very disappointing result.	A lot of production problems at the start of the year.

Second explanation

High level of competition.

Now listen to model versions on tape B3.2.

C How to organise the information – Signposting the route

C1 Focus

In longer presentations it is very important to make the structure of your presentation clear to the audience. One way to do this is to *signpost* the different parts of the presentation, showing where each main part begins and ends.

Study the plan below. It shows the structure of the presentation for Aqua-Sparkle.

Presentation plan

Part 1	Market Overview
Part 2	Brand performance of Aqua-Sparkle
Point 1	Sales performance in three types of outlets
	a. National Grocers
	b. Independent Grocers
	c. Neighbourhood Stores
Point 2	Profitability of brand
Part 3	Outlook for the future

Listen to tape C1. You will hear the presenter giving the presentation about Aqua-Sparkle.

Notice the phrases and sentences the presenter uses to introduce each main part of the presentation and to move from point to point.

Complete the phrases and sentences following the notes on the right.

Phrases and sentences	Notes
.... an overview of the total market for lemonade drinks ...	*Introduces the first part – market overview*
.... the brand performance of Aqua-Sparkle ...	*Moves to the second part – brand performance*
.... , that's the .... for Aqua-Sparkle, and .... the brand's performance in each of the three types of retail outlet ...	*Summarises and moves to first point – performance in different outlets*
.... , ... the profitability of the brand? ...	*Moves to the second point – profitability*

.... , ... my
overview of the current situation, and

Summarises and moves to third part – the outlook

....

.... the outlook …

Check your answers in the key **C1**

C2 Summary

Signposting the route through a presentation

- In a longer presentation it is useful to signpost the presentation to show where one part ends and a new one starts.
  This helps to orientate the audience by making the structure of the presentation clearer to follow.

- Here are some useful phrases and sentences.
  I'll begin by … (+ verb in the …*ing* form)
  Let's start with … (+ noun)
  If I could now turn to …
  My next point is …
  Now, turning to …
  Now, what about … ?
  Let me now move on to …

Using summaries

- Particularly in longer presentations include summaries.
- Give them at the end of major parts of your presentation or after a key point.
- Use them as check points to summarise or draw a conclusion before you move on to a new point.
  So that's the general picture for … and now let's look at …
  That completes my overview of … so now I'd like to move on to …

C3 Tasks

I. The plan below is for a presentation reviewing performance of chocolate products. Study the plan.

Presentation plan

Part 1	Levels of chocolate consumption.
Part 2	Performance of three product segments.

Point 1	Performance of two segments:
	    chocolate bars.
	    boxes of chocolates.

Point 2	Performance of bags segment.
Part 3	Outlook for the future.

a. Complete the phrases the presenter uses to make the structure of her presentation clear to the audience. Match the phrases below 1–5 with phrases i–v.

Follow the example.

1. Now turning to	i. our two top performing segments.
	ii. and now I'll move on to the outlook for the future.
2. That gives you an overview of how the three product segments have performed,	iii. the performance of our three product segments, in terms of market share.
3. I'll start with	iv. the remaining segment, bags of chocolate.
4. Before analysing the performance over the last 12 months,	v. I'd like to give you some facts about levels of chocolate consumption.
5. So now, if we could look at	

b. Look at the presentation plan above. Put the sentences in the correct order for the presentation.

Check your answers in the key **C3.1**

2. The plan on page 29 is for a presentation in which the presenter informs the audience about how her company selects and orientates employees for overseas jobs. Study the plan.

Presentation plan

Part 1	Costs of sending our people to work abroad.
Part 2	Reasons why so many people come back before the end of their contracts.
Summary	Given high costs – very important to choose right kind of person.
Part 3	Characteristics of a good assignee.
Point 1	Personal attributes.
Point 2	Type of work experience which is useful for jobs abroad.
Summary	Completes the picture of kind of person we are looking for.
Part 4	Our selection and orientation procedures.

Listen to tape C3.2.

You will hear six instructions asking you to introduce the different parts and points in the presentation. Make your response after each instruction.

You will then hear a model version.

Example

Instruction 1   Introduce the first part of the presentation

Your response   ....

Model version   **Let me start with some facts about the costs of sending our people to work abroad.**

D How to create interest – Using rhetorical questions

D1 Focus

A useful device for involving the audience in your presentation is to ask rhetorical questions, questions which the presenter does not expect the audience to answer.

Listen to tape D1. You will hear an extract from another version of the presentation about Aqua-Sparkle.

In this version the information is the same, but the presenter includes rhetorical questions to link some of the points he is making.

What rhetorical questions does the presenter use to connect these points?

Follow the example.

Point 1	Point 2	Rhetorical question
The solid performance in the National Grocers sector.	The reason	*How can we explain this?*
a. The poor performance of the Independent Grocers and the delisting of Aqua-Sparkle by some customers.	The reason	....
b. The fact that Aqua-Sparkle is priced higher than the competition.	The solution	....

Check your answers in the key **D1**

D2 Summary

Using rhetorical questions

- Rhetorical questions are useful devices. They give one-way communication the appearance of a dialogue with the audience.

- Use rhetorical questions to:
  build links between the various points in your presentation.
  help keep the audience interested.
  make the audience feel involved in your presentation.

- Here are some examples of rhetorical questions:

Sales are down on last year.	What's the explanation for this? How can we explain this? What can we do about it? How will this affect us? What are the implications for the company?

D3 Tasks

1. Use a rhetorical question to link the ideas below.

Follow the example. You may need to rephrase the wording in the second idea.

Example

a. **Idea 1** Recently there's been a surge in European sales to Japan.
   Idea 2 This increase reflects Japanese affluence and a recently acquired taste for luxury cars and designer label products.

Recently there's been a surge in European sales to Japan. Why is this? Firstly, it reflects Japanese affluence. And secondly, a recently acquired taste for luxury cars and designer label products.

b. **Idea 1** With the downturn in the US car market, our sales have dropped considerably.
   Idea 2 One solution would be to reduce production.

Check your answers in the key **D3.1**

2. Listen to tape D3.2 You will hear model versions of the last exercise.

Notice how the presenter pauses slightly after each rhetorical question.

S/He does this to create impact and give his/her audience just enough time to think about the answer to the question. S/He does not expect an actual answer.

3. The notes below are from two different presentations.

How would you connect the ideas in each set of notes? Include rhetorical questions as links between the different ideas.

If possible record your answers.

a.

Notes from presentation 1

Project now two months behind schedule.

Reason
1. Bad weather conditions in the early part of the year.
2. Problems with our main sub-contractor.

b.

Notes from presentation 2

Last week another accident in our bottling plant in France.
Nobody hurt / production held up for two days / cost company a lot of money.

Action to prevent further accidents
1. Check all equipment.
2. Improve safety procedures.

Now listen to tape D3.3. You will hear the two sets of notes developed as extracts from presentations. Compare your versions with the versions on the tape.

Contrasting statements of fact and comments

4. Listen to tape D3.4.

You will hear three short extracts from the presentation about Aqua-Sparkle. In each of the extracts in the table on page 32 the presenter gives some facts about the performance of Aqua-Sparkle and then comments on it.

Notice how the presenter pauses before commenting on the facts he is giving.

He does this to help his audience differentiate between purely factual analysis and his more subjective comments.

Fact / Trend	Comment
a. ... several customers have actually delisted Aqua-Sparkle,	which is a very worrying trend.
b. ... can be attributed to the recent sales drive in the area.	And we're confident that the performance is finally beginning to turn around.
c. ... we are, in fact, ahead of our target.	This is clearly a very encouraging result.

5. Explain the trends below and add comments. Make sure you pause in the correct place to distinguish the factual information from the personal comment.

Follow the example. The pause is marked ☐ .

 If possible record yourself.

Fact / Trend	Comment
Launch the BX40 next month.	Confident turn performance round.

The BX40 will be launched next month ☐ And we are confident it will turn our performance round.

a. The car market still buoyant.	Surprising considering the economic climate.
b. Sales off target by eight per cent.	Very disappointing result.
c. The plan is to trial the drug in September.	We feel too soon.

Now listen to tape D3.5. You will hear presenters describe the facts and trends and comment on them.

E Activities

1. Stage 1

Choose one of the topics below.

> ~ Safety systems ~ Transport ~ Energy ~ Advertising ~ Magazines
> ~ Business travel ~ Competition ~ Office design

Stage 2

Brainstorm the topic. Make brief notes of any ideas which come into your head.

Stage 3

Your purpose is to inform the audience on an aspect of the topic. Decide on the theme and main points for the presentation.

Stage 4

Decide how to develop the points to give a clear shape to the presentation. Include transitional phrases or sentences to make the structure of your presentation clear.

Stage 5

 Give the presentation. If possible record yourself.

Use the checklist below to help you evaluate your presentation.

CHECKLIST

	Yes/No	Example phrases

Did you:

- State the purpose of the presentation?
- Signpost the points to be developed?
- Make it clear where the main points in the presentation start and end?
- Use summaries to make the link between what has gone before and what is to follow?

2. Choose one of the frameworks as a basis for your own presentation.

a. **Topic – Project update**

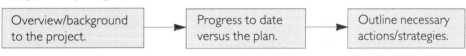

| Overview/background to the project. | → | Progress to date versus the plan. | → | Outline necessary actions/strategies. |

b. **Topic – Product performance review**

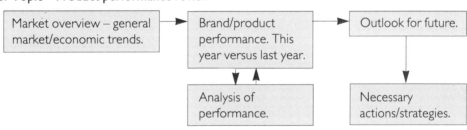

| Market overview – general market/economic trends. | → | Brand/product performance. This year versus last year. | → | Outlook for future. |

| | | Analysis of performance. | | Necessary actions/strategies. |

Answer key

A Preparation

1. poor/disappointing
2. the North
3. below
4. National Grocers
5. 13

B What to say

B1 🎧
Extract 1

PRESENTER: A key area of concern is the southern region where purchases **have dropped by** 14 per cent. **The main explanation for this** decline **is** reduced disposable income in this area **due to** very high interest rates, **and also to** high commitments on mortgages and other types of loans.

Extract 2

PRESENTER: … and now let's look at the brand's performance in each of the three types of outlet. First, the National Grocers. This sector **has shown** the **most solid performance** with a **considerable improvement on** last year. A **particular reason for this is** the one-pack promotional campaign within National Grocers, which is clearly having the desired effect on sales.

Extract 3

PRESENTER: In the second sector, Independent Grocers, the brand **performed badly**. As you can see, the rate of sales **is well down on** last year, and several customers have actually delisted Aqua-Sparkle, which is obviously a very worrying trend. **The key problem** here **is** price. Competitors have been discounting heavily with a **consequent reduction** in retail shelf-price. This means that now, in this sector, Aqua-Sparkle is priced much higher than the competition.

Extract 4

PRESENTER: … gross profit **is showing good growth** with the profit per litre up 2.7p on last year. **There are** two **reasons** for **this. First**, a better control of discounts. As I said, we're deliberately not discounting in order to maintain the premium positioning of the brand. **Second**, we've managed to achieve a reduction in packaging costs.

B1

See tapescript B1 above. The missing words are in **bold**.

B3.1 Model version

a. Japan is performing ahead of the market.
b. The performance of the UK market has been disappointing with an increase of just four per cent on last year/with sales up by only four per cent on last year.
c. The US/US market performed poorly with a slight increase of only/just two per cent.

B3.2 🎧 Model versions
Point 1

PRESENTER: There's been a slight decrease in chocolate consumption. One reason for this is a general change in eating habits, with a move away from sweet things. Another reason is increasing pressure from health lobbies.

Point 2

PRESENTER: The market for boxes of chocolates is always very difficult. This is mainly because it's a seasonal market, with major sales around Christmas, but a much lower volume of sales for the rest of the year.

Point 3

PRESENTER: Sales for bags of chocolates were well below target, which is very disappointing. There are two reasons for this poor result. First, we had a lot of production problems at the start of the year. Second, the high level of competition.

C How to organise the information

C1 🔊

PRESENTER: **I'd like to start with** an overview of the total market for lemonade drinks. If you look at this chart you can see lemonade continues to perform poorly with consumer purchases down by seven per cent across the country. And you can also see that lemonade continues to perform worse than the fizzy drinks market as a whole, which is only down three per cent. A key area of concern is the southern region where purchases have dropped by 14 per cent. The main explanation for this decline is reduced disposable income in this area due to very high interest rates, and also to high commitments on mortgages and other types of loans. At the moment the north is outperforming the market as a whole, down only one per cent. But, the fact is, this region only accounts for 12 per cent of our lemonade sales. So, the overall performance of the lemonade category has not been very good and, unfortunately, the general outlook is no better with declines likely to continue well into next year.

Let me now turn to the brand performance of Aqua-Sparkle and look at our six months' sales performance in different types of outlet – National Grocers, Independent Grocers and Neighbourhood Stores. Looking at the chart now you'll see that, at first glance, the performance for the first part of the year is disappointing with sales three per cent down on plan, especially against last year's performance when the brand showed a one per cent increase. But in fact, this three per cent decrease is a considerably better performance than the lemonade category as a whole, which you'll remember, was seven per cent down on last year. **So,** that's the **general picture** for Aqua-Sparkle, and **now let's look at** the brand's performance in each of the three types of retail outlet.

First, the National Grocers. This sector has shown the most solid performance with a considerable improvement on last year. A particular reason is the one-pack promotional campaign within National Grocers, which is clearly having the desired effect on sales.

In the second sector, Independent Grocers, the brand performed badly. As you can see, the rate of sales is well down on last year, and several customers have actually delisted Aqua-Sparkle, which is a very worrying trend. The key problem here is price. Competitors have been discounting heavily with a consequent reduction in retail shelf-price. This means that now, in this sector, Aqua-Sparkle is priced much higher than the competition. One obvious solution would be to follow the lead of our competitors and discount Aqua-Sparkle, but we have decided not to do this as it would affect the brand's premium positioning, which we want to maintain. So in this particular sector, Independent Grocers, we can see further declines being likely.

That leaves the final sector which is Neighbourhood Stores. Here the sales for the year so far are five per cent behind the plan and two per cent behind the equivalent period for last year. But this result is not as disappointing as it first appears, and in fact represents a one per cent improvement on the first quarter. This slight improvement can be attributed to the recent sales drive in the area. And we're confident that the performance is finally beginning to turn around.

Now, what about the profitability of the brand? As this chart shows, in spite of some of the problems I've mentioned, gross profit is showing good growth with the profit per litre up 2.7p on last year. There are two reasons for this. First, better control of discounts. As I said, we're deliberately not discounting in order to maintain the premium positioning of the brand. Second, we've managed to achieve a reduction in packaging costs. So, if you look at our total gross profit, you'll see that we are, in fact, eight per cent ahead of our target. This is clearly a very encouraging result.

So, that completes my overview of the current situation and, **now I'd like to move on to** the outlook for the future of the market as a whole, and Aqua-Sparkle in particular.

C1

See tapescript C1 above. The missing words are in **bold.**

C3.1

a. 1. iv 2. ii 3. i 4. v 5. iii
b. 4 5 3 1 2

C3.2 🔊

Instruction 1   Introduce the first part of the presentation.

Your response   ....

Model version   **Let me start with some facts about the costs of sending our people to work abroad.**

Instruction 2	Move to the second part of the presentation.
Your response	....
Model version	**Now, let's look at the reasons why so many of our people come back before the end of their contracts.**
Instruction 3	Give an interim summary and move onto the third part of the presentation.
Your response	....
Model version	**Given the high costs, it's obviously very important to choose the right kind of person for an overseas job. So, now I'd like to talk about what makes a good assignee.**
Instruction 4	Move to the first point.
Your response	....
Model version	**First, what about personal attributes?**
Instruction 5	Move to the second point.
Your response	....
Model version	**My second point is about the type of work experience, which is useful for jobs abroad.**
Instruction 6	Give an interim summary and move to the final part
Your response	....
Model version	**That completes the picture of the kind of person we're looking for, so let me now explain our selection and orientation procedures.**

D How to create interest

D1

a. So, what's the reason for the disappointing performance?
b. What can we do about this?

D1 🔲

So that's the general picture for Aqua-Sparkle, and now what about the brand's performance in the three types of retail outlet? First, the National Grocers. This sector has shown the most solid performance with a considerable improvement on last year. **How can we explain this?** A particular reason is the one-pack promotional campaign within National Grocers, which is clearly having the desired effect on sales. In the second sector, Independent Grocers, the brand performed badly. As you can see, the rate of sales is well down on last year, and several customers have actually delisted Aqua-Sparkle, which is a very worrying trend. **So, what's the reason for the disappointing performance?** The key problem here is price. Competitors have been discounting heavily with a consequent reduction in retail shelf-price. This means that now, in this sector, Aqua-Sparkle is priced much higher than the competition.

What can we do about this? One obvious solution would be to follow the lead of our competitors and discount Aqua-Sparkle, but we've decided not to do this as it would affect the brand's premium positioning, which we want to maintain.

D3.1 Model version

a. Recently there's been a surge in European sales to Japan. Why is that? Firstly, it reflects Japanese affluence. And secondly, a recently acquired taste for luxury cars and designer label products.

   Other rhetorical questions: What's the explanation/reason? How can we explain this dramatic/rapid increase?

b. With the downturn in the US car market, our sales have dropped considerably. What can we do about this? One solution would be to reduce production.

   Other rhetorical questions: What's the solution (to this)?

D3.2 🔲

See key D3.1 above for the full tapescript.

D3.3 🔲 Model version

a. The project is now running two months behind schedule. What is the reason for the delay? It's mainly due to the bad weather conditions in the early part of the year. And also to the problems we've had with our main sub-contractor.

b. Last week we had yet another accident in our bottling plant in France. Fortunately nobody was hurt, but production was held up for two days, which cost the company a lot of money. What can we do to prevent further accidents? First, we need to check all the equipment. And then look at ways of improving our safety procedures.

D3.4 🔲

a. As you can see, the rate of sales is well down on last year, and several customers have actually delisted Aqua-Sparkle, which is a very worrying trend.

b. This slight improvement can be attributed to the recent sales drive in the area. And we're confident that the performance is finally beginning to turn around.

c. So, if we look at our total gross profit, you'll see that we are, in fact, ahead of our target. This is clearly a very encouraging result.

D3.5 🔲

The BX 40 will be launched next month ☐ . And we are confident it will turn our performance round.

a. The car market is still buoyant ☐ which is surprising considering the economic climate.

b. Sales were off target by eight per cent ☐ which is a very disappointing result.

or

Sales were off target by eight per cent. ☐ This is a very disappointing result.

c. The plan is to trial the drug in September. ☐ We feel that's too soon.

or

The plan is to trial the drug in September ☐ which we feel is too soon.

The persuasive presentation

A	Preparation
B	What to say	Building arguments
C	How to organise the information	Talking through options
D	How to create interest	Emphasising and highlighting key points
E	Activities

A Preparation

Three months ago an American company, Marcon Chemicals, asked the LX Consulting Group to look at their computer activity in Europe.

At the moment Marcon has ten data centres in Europe, with a total staff of 60.

Seven of these data centres are at the head offices of their European subsidiaries, and run administrative systems. The other three are at various European plants and run manufacturing systems.

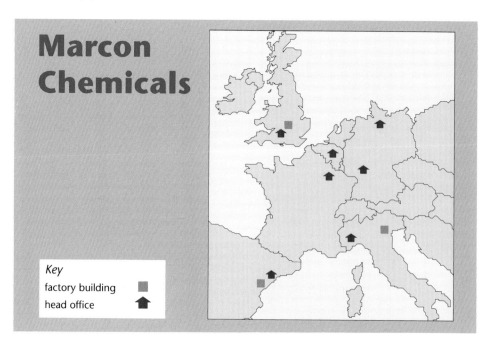

Marcon Chemicals

Key
factory building
head office

I. What are the benefits and weaknesses of this type of decentralised organisation?
List the benefits and weaknesses below.

Benefits	Weaknesses

Check your answers in the key   AI

B What to say – Building arguments

The main purpose of many presentations is to *persuade* the audience e.g. you want the audience to accept your plan, or a change in procedure. In this type of presentation it is very important to build convincing arguments.

B1 Focus

The head of the LX team is preparing a presentation summarising the results of the study.

Context	A meeting at Marcon chemicals.
Audience	Key managers from the different European subsidiaries.
Purpose	To persuade the audience that her consultancy's recommendations are the right ones.

Listen to tape B1.

You will hear five extracts from the first part of the presentation. The presenter is assessing the current organisation of the company's computer activity in Europe.

Notice the different ways she builds up her arguments to convince the audience of the need for change.

Complete the missing words in each extract. Then read the notes below.

Follow the example.

Extract 1 – The presenter explains the benefits of the current organisation for the user.

Advantages   *Because* .... each data centre needs to be self-sufficient and provide a full range of services, there's a greater variety of work, and a constant need for the updating of skills.

Effect   .... a range of challenging jobs and a high level of job satisfaction …

Notice how the presenter simply states the factual relationship between cause and effect.

Extract 2 – The presenter balances her argument by showing the disadvantages of the current organisation.

Disadvantages .... , a major drawback is the vast amount of
duplication... Duplication of both equipment and skills ...

.... you have a lot of people doing the
same jobs in different locations,

Effect there's a great waste of resources. .... , ... ,
maintaining this level of duplication has a ....
.... on the company.

Notice how the presenter again shows a factual relationship between cause and effect.

Extract 3 – The presenter summarises the situation.

Advantages .... the present organisation of your computing
facilities offers some benefits,

Disadvantages it obviously isn't working to maximum efficiency.
.... , it's costing the company a lot of money.

Implied consequence *There is a need for change.*

Notice how the presenter states both advantages and disadvantages, and indicates an implied, but unstated consequence.

Extract 4 – The presenter argues the case for change in the organisation of the administrative data centres.

Facts ... a great deal of time and money has been spent on developing
new administrative systems, ... today
management's needs are largely catered for. ....
.... , at the plant level,
business is evolving rapidly and there's a growing need for more
sophisticated computer applications.

Consequence It's .... that you need to shift
resources from administration to manufacturing systems
development.

Notice how she builds up her arguments step by step to achieve the desired conclusion.

Extract 5 – The presenter makes her final recommendation.

Summary .... the trends I've just outlined,

Recommendations we propose that you leave the manufacturing data
centres as they are. .... , we see a major need
for consolidation in the administrative data centres.

Notice how the presenter summarises before she gives her recommendation.

Check your answers in the key **BI**

B2 Summary

Building arguments

- Highlight the relationship between the different points you want to make by using connecting words, e.g.
  - to show a different argument
    however, on the other hand, although, in spite of this
  - to show a consequence,
    therefore, so, consequently, because of this, as a result
  - to show an additional argument,
    moreover, in addition to this, not only … but also…

- Using connecting words like these will help:
  - you to build convincing arguments.
  - your audience to follow your arguments, and anticipate the direction you are moving in.

- A frequent tactic in persuasive presentations is to point out the relationship between cause and effect. You can do this by:
  - showing the factual relationship between cause and effect. (Extracts I and 2 in BI)
  - setting out the facts so that they strongly imply a consequence, but without stating it directly. (Extract 3)
  - setting out facts so that they strongly argue for doing something, e.g. directly arguing the case for change. (Extract 4)
  - summarising and making recommendations for action. (Extract 5)

B3 Tasks

I. The points below are from a presentation about a staffing problem.

Connect the points, following the instructions and the example below.

Show a factual relationship between cause and effect.

Point I   There has been a 20 per cent increase in business.

Point 2   The work load has increased considerably.

Over the last six months there's been a 20 per cent increase in our business. And, as a result, the work load has increased considerably.

a. Show a factual relationship between cause and effect.

  Point I There has been a substantial increase in the business.

  Point 2 Staff are working a considerable amount of overtime.

b. Build up the arguments to show an implied but unstated consequence – customer service has deteriorated

  Point I The sales team have to spend so much of their day on extra administration.

  Point 2 They have less time for customer service.

c. Argue the case for change – the recruitment of extra staff.

  Point I If we recruit extra staff, our costs will increase.

  Point 2 If we do nothing, we will certainly lose staff.

  Point 3 We cannot afford to lose good staff whom we have spent years training.

Check your answers in the key B3.1

2. The notes below are from a presentation about a British company's policy of posting personnel to foreign subsidiaries.

Choose suitable connecting words to show an alternative argument.

Follow the example.

Expensive to send people from the UK to work in foreign subsidiaries/to remain competitive we must have people with international experience.

It's very expensive to send people from the UK to work in foreign subsidiaries. **However,** *if we want to remain competitive we must have people with international experience.*

a. We have many people with the right business background/not everybody adapts well to cultural change.

b. There are advantages in having people from headquarters going to work abroad/more and more people are coming back from assignments before end of contracts.

Check your answers in the key **B3.2**

3. Expand the following notes by choosing connecting words to show additional arguments, and make a recommendation.

Follow the example.

Duplication of equipment in the two centres/duplication of skills/consolidating the centres into one.

Not only is there a duplication of equipment in the two centres, but there is also a duplication of skills. We therefore recommend consolidating the centres into one.

a. Harder to keep people in overseas posts/increasingly difficult to recruit people to go abroad/review our terms and conditions.

b. Necessary for people to have the right experience/be able to adapt to new environments and working conditions/proper training and orientation before going abroad.

Check your answers in the key **B3.3**

C How to organise the information – Talking through options

C1 Focus

 Listen to tape C1.

You will now hear the presenter's recommendations for Marcon's European administrative data centres. The LX Consulting group looked at three options.

Notice how the presenter explains all three options, not just the case for the preferred solution. She does this to show that the subject has been studied in detail.

Notice the expressions and sentences the presenter uses to explain the different options, and to move from point to point.

Complete the missing words in the extract, then read the notes on the right.

Extract 1

In fact, ...

States the options

three different ....

.... , ... run all your computing
from three regional centres, ...

States first option

So, ... benefits of
this option?
First, you'd achieve a reduction ...

Moves to the benefits

.... , ... , some practical

*Moves to the
weaknesses*

.... , that would make it very difficult to implement
this solution. First, the question of ...

Extract 2

So, the second ....

*Moves on to the
second option*

.... to expand one ...

The .... benefit in this ....

*States the main
benefit*

.... full optimisation of your
computer resources ...

.... , there are .... here ....
If you expanded Bristol, Barcelona, or indeed Frankfurt you
would have even greater space problems.

Moves to weaknesses

Extract 3

.... , ...

*Moves to preferred
option*

.... the third option, to organise ...

Now, ... , this seems

States a weakness

to be a more expensive .... in terms of the cost per
computing hour.

.... the .... very

*Balances the
weakness with
benefits*

....

Check your answers in the key `CI`

C2 Summary

Outlining options

- If there are alternatives to your proposal, explain them. This will show that you have looked at different ways of dealing with the situation.

- Here are some useful expressions for explaining options.
  We've considered / looked at three options.
  One way to solve this problem is ... Another is to ...
  There are two alternatives ...
  The first option is to ...
  But what about the second option?
  So, now let's look at the third option, which is to ...

- Outline both weaknesses and benefits for each of the options you consider. Here are some useful expressions introducing weaknesses and benefits.

What are the benefits?	*There are, however, disadvantages ...*
Now, what about the advantages?	*But there are some problems too.*
Now, I'd like to look at the benefits.	*On the other hand ...*

- If there is a series of benefits or weaknesses, make it clear which are your strongest points, and which are just secondary.

C3 Tasks

1. You are the Personnel Manager at one of the subsidiaries of an American bank. Recently your bank has seen a major increase in its foreign loans business with the result that staff are working overtime on a frequent basis.

   The notes below are from a presentation in which you explain two different solutions to the problem.

   Study the two sets of notes for the presentation.

Solution 1: Recruit temporary staff

Benefits
- Reduction in amount of overtime
- More flexibility if downturn in business

Weakness
- Permanent staff will have to spend a lot of their time training temporary staff

---

Solution 2: Recruit extra permanent staff

Benefit — Major opportunity to create an effective team of specialists

Weaknesses — Expensive
— Lose flexibilty to adapt to changing market conditions

Note: Your preference is for the second solution.

Listen to tape C3.1.

You will hear eight instructions asking you to:
— outline the two possible solutions to the staffing problem.
— argue the case for each solution.

Make your response after each instruction. You will then hear a model version.

Example

Instruction 1   Outline the solutions you've considered.

Your response   ....

Model version 1   **We've looked at two possible solutions to the problem.**

D How to create interest – Emphasising and highlighting key points

D I Focus

Listen to tape D I.

You will hear extracts from another version of the presentation about the data centres, which the LX consultant gives to a different audience.

In these extracts the presenter highlights and emphasises her points to give them more impact.

Four of her points are summarised below. As you listen, complete the words she uses to state the points. Then read the notes below.

Point 1 A major drawback is the vast amount of duplication which is going on in the data centres, duplication of systems time, equipment and skills.

Her words A major drawback is the vast amount of duplication which is going on in the data

centres – .... systems time, ...

equipment, and .... ,

.... skills.

Notice how she repeats the word *duplication* to reinforce the idea.

Point 2 Although the present organisation of your computing facilities offers some benefits, it isn't working to maximum efficiency.

Her words Although the present organisation of your computing facilities offers some

benefits, it .... working to maximum efficiency.

Notice how she emphasises the word *not*.

Point 3 We don't see any need for change in the manufacturing data centres, and we propose that you leave them as they are. However, we see a need for change in the administrative data centres.

Her words We .... need for change in the manufacturing data centres, and we propose that you leave them as they are. However, we

.... a major need for a change in the administrative data centres.

Notice how she places emphasis on the word *no*, and notice also the use of *do* to give emphasis.

Point 4 So, now let's look at the third option, to organise a new data centre for European operations. We aren't suggesting that you build your own centre. Our proposal is that you sub-contract all your administrative computing requirements to a computer services company.

Her words So, now let's look at the third option, to organise a new data centre for

European operations. .... suggesting that you build your

own data centre. That would be too expensive. But ....

.... proposing .... that you sub-contract all your administrative computing requirements to a computer services company.

Notice how she highlights her proposal by beginning with the word *what*.

Check your answers in the key **D I**

D2 Summary

Highlighting information

There are a number of different ways you can emphasise and highlight key points in your presentation to give it more impact, and to sound more persuasive. Here are some of them.

- Stressing an auxiliary verb.
  You can highlight key ideas by stressing auxiliary verbs like *is, was, were, will, has*.
  With negatives put the stress on words like *no* or *not* eg: *is **not*** or *will **not***

It's costing a lot of money.	BECOMES	*It **is** costing a lot of money.*
We aren't recommending any major changes.		*We are **not** recommending any major changes.*
The company doesn't see any need for change.		*The company sees **no** need for change.*

- Adding the auxiliary *do, does* or *did* in an affirmative sentence.

  You can emphasise an idea by adding the word *do, does* or *did* just in front of the verb.

We see a need for change.	BECOMES	*We **do** see a need for change.*
Personnel knew about it before.		*Personnel **did** know about it before.*
I think it's very expensive.		*I **do** think it's very expensive.*

- Changing the normal word order of a sentence

We're suggesting cuts in production.	BECOMES	*What we're suggesting are cuts in production.*
They propose a major reorganisation.		*What they propose is a major reorganisation.*
More investment is needed not cuts in investment.		*What is needed is more investment not cuts in investment.*

- Repeating key words and ideas
  Repeating important ideas or vocabulary is also a useful way of reinforcing a point.

We need to reduce production and packaging costs.	BECOMES	*We need to reduce production costs, and we also need to reduce packaging costs.*

Now listen to tape D2. You will hear the examples from the summary. Notice where the presenters pause and how they create emphasis.

D3 Tasks

1. Listen to tape D3.1

You will hear the extract from a presentation about the overtime problem in one of the branches of a big American bank.

Notice how the presenter gives emphasis to his main points.

Mark the extract to show where the presenter pauses.

> ### Extract
>
> As we've seen, we do have serious staff problems in our international loans department. So, what I'm proposing is to recruit two full-time staff. What are the benefits? First, it will improve the morale in the department. Second, it'll produce a more stable team. Third, it'll give our staff more time for handling each loan application, and so improve our customer service.

Check your answers in the key **D3.1**

2. How would you change these statements to make them sound stronger and more convincing?

Follow the example.

a. There isn't any need to change the date of the product launch.
   There's *no* need to change the date of the product launch.

b. We can keep our sales and administration departments separate, but we need to have them in one location.

c. Maintaining a separate research centre in Milan isn't an effective solution.

d. Our proposal is to relocate all research and development to our factory in Frankfurt.

e. Building the plant in Spain has clear advantages. It will give us a foothold in Spain, access to a skilled workforce and a new factory, and all at a relatively low cost.

Now listen to the model versions on tape D3.2.

E Activities

Choose one of the frameworks below as the basis for a presentation. If possible, record yourself and play it back.

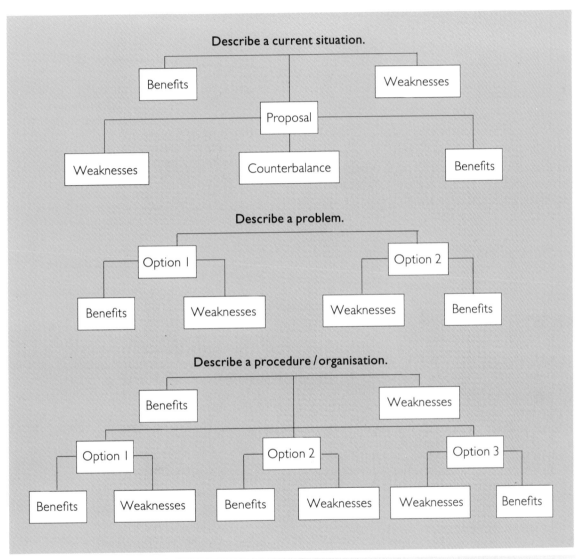

Describe a current situation.

- Benefits
- Weaknesses
- Proposal
  - Weaknesses
  - Counterbalance
  - Benefits

Describe a problem.

- Option 1
  - Benefits
  - Weaknesses
- Option 2
  - Weaknesses
  - Benefits

Describe a procedure / organisation.

- Benefits
- Weaknesses
  - Option 1
    - Benefits
    - Weaknesses
  - Option 2
    - Benefits
    - Weaknesses
  - Option 3
    - Weaknesses
    - Benefits

CHECKLIST

	Yes/No	Examples

- Evaluate the *organisation* of your presentation.
  - Have you used signals to move from point to point?
  - Have you used connecting words to make your arguments clear?
- Evaluate your *delivery*.
  - Have you emphasised and highlighted your main ideas?
  - Are there any changes you need to make?

Answer key

A Preparation

Model version

Benefits

Able to provide service at a local level.

Better understanding of local needs.

Because each centre has to offer the full range of services, there is a variety of work for systems staff.

High level of job satisfaction and motivation amongst the staff.

Weaknesses

Staffing problems at small data centres e.g. in holiday time. Very small centres may find it hard to offer a fully comprehensive service.

High level of duplication e.g. equipment, skills.

High cost.

B What to say

B1

Extract 1

PRESENTER: There are certain advantages for the systems staff. **Because** each data centre needs to be self-sufficient and provide a full range of services, there's a greater variety of work, and a constant need for the updating of skills. **The result is** a range of challenging jobs and a high level of job satisfaction and motivation among the computer staff.

Extract 2

PRESENTER: **However**, a major drawback is the vast amount of duplication which is going on in the data centres. Duplication of both equipment and skills. The fact that you provide support for all your users means that you need to maintain the same equipment in each data centre. Equally, you also need people with the same skills in each place. **And because** you have a lot of people doing the same jobs in different locations, there's a great waste of resources. **So, clearly,** maintaining this level of

duplication has **a negative cost impact** on the company.

Extract 3

PRESENTER: So, to summarise. **Although** the present organisation of your computing facilities offers some benefits, it obviously isn't working to maximum efficiency. **Moreover**, it's costing the company a lot of money.

Extract 4

PRESENTER: Over the last ten years a great deal of time and money has been spent on developing new administrative systems, **and so** today management's needs are largely catered for. **On the other hand**, at the plant level, business is evolving rapidly and there's a growing need for more sophisticated computer applications. It's **because of this** that you need to shift resources from administration to manufacturing systems development.

Extract 5

PRESENTER: **Given** the trends I've just outlined, we propose that you leave the manufacturing data centres as they are. **However**, we see a major need for consolidation in the administrative data centres.

B1

See tapescript B1 above. The missing words are in **bold**.

B3.1 Model version

a. There's been a substantial increase in business. And because of that, staff are working a lot of overtime.

b. Because the sales team have to spend so much of their day on extra administrative tasks, they have less time for customer service.

c. If we recruit extra staff our costs will increase. On the other hand, if we do nothing we'll certainly lose good staff. And clearly, we cannot afford to lose these people whom we've spent years training.

B3.2 Model version

a. **Although** we have many people with the right business background, not everybody adapts well to cultural change.

b. There are advantages in having people from headquarters going to work abroad. **On the other hand**, more and more people are coming back from assignments before the end of their contracts.

B3.3 Model version

a. It's becoming harder and harder to keep people in overseas posts. And moreover, it's becoming increasingly difficult to recruit people. So we recommend a review of terms and conditions.

b. It's necessary for people to have the right kind of experience. And they must also be able to adapt to a new environment and working conditions. So we recommend that everyone is given proper training and orientation before going abroad.

C *How to organise the information*

C1 🖭

PRESENTER: So, for the rest of this presentation I'll be talking about the options we've considered for consolidating the administrative data centres. In fact, **we've looked at** three different **options. First, to** run all your computing from three regional centres, one in Bristol for the UK, one in Barcelona for Southern Europe, and one in Frankfurt for the rest of Europe. So, **what are the** benefits of this option?

First, you'd achieve a reduction in the number of data centres from seven to three. And, at the same time you'd also keep a relatively high level of decentralisation so that you could continue to provide high quality end-user support.

There are, however, some practical **problems** that would make it very difficult to implement this solution. First, the question of what to do with the staff from the data centres which would be closed down. Second, there are serious space problems in Bristol and Barcelona. Third, and most seriously, you wouldn't achieve the full optimisation you're aiming at because you'd still have some problems of duplication.

So, the second **option we considered was** to expand one of the existing regional administrative data centres. The **major** benefit in this **case would be** full optimisation of your computer resources. It would maximise your use of manpower, eliminate duplication, and result in clear cost savings.

But there are **problems** here **too**.

If you expanded Bristol, Barcelona, or indeed Frankfurt, you would have even greater space problems. But the real disadvantage is the length of time it would take to carry out the change from seven data centres down to just one.

So, now let's look at the third option, to organise a new data centre for European operations. We aren't suggesting that you build your own centre. That would be too expensive. Our proposal is that you sub-contract all your administrative computing requirements to an outside computer services company. Now, **on the surface**, this seems to be a more expensive **option** in terms of the cost per computing hour.

But the **benefits are** very **clear**. You'll achieve all the advantages of full optimisation – a more efficient use of resources and manpower – which will result in considerable savings in the long term. But the main benefit is the time it would take to implement the change. We estimate that with this option complete changeover can be achieved in just a year.

C1

See tapescript C1 above. The missing words are in **bold**.

C3.1 🖭

Instruction 1	Outline the solutions you've considered.
Your response	....
Model version	**We've looked at two possible solutions to the problem.**
Instruction 2	Outline the first solution.
Your response	....
Model version	**The first solution is to recruit temporary staff.**
Instruction 3	Move on to the benefits and state them.
Your response	....
Model version	**What are the advantages? First, we will reduce the amount of overtime for our permanent staff. Another advantage – it will give us more flexibility if there's a downturn in business.**
Instruction 4	Move on to the weakness and state it.
Your response	....
Model version	**But there's a problem too. If we employ a lot of temporary staff, our permanent people will need to spend a lot of their time training them.**

Instruction 5 — Move on to the second solution and outline it.

Your response — ....

Model version — **So, let's look at the second solution which is to recruit extra permanent staff.**

Instruction 6 — Move on to the weaknesses and state them.

Your response — ....

Model version — **With this option there are some disadvantages. It will be more expensive. And we'll also lose some of our flexibility to adapt to changing market conditions.**

Instruction 7 — Counterbalance these weaknesses by stating the benefit.

Your response — ....

Model version — **On the other hand, recruiting permanent staff will give us a major opportunity to create a really effective team of specialists.**

D How to create interest

D1

Extract 1

A major drawback is the vast amount of duplication which is going on in the data centres – **duplication of** systems time, **duplication of** equipment, and **last but not least, duplication of** skills.

Extract 2

Although the present organisation of your computing facilities offers some benefits, it **is not** working to maximum efficiency.

Extract 3

We **can see no** need for change in the manufacturing data centres, and we propose that you leave them as they are. However, we **do see** a major need for a change in the administrative data centres.

Extract 4

So, now let's look at the third option, to organise a new data centre for European operations. **We're not** suggesting that you build your own data centre. That would be too expensive. But **what we are** proposing **is** that you sub-contract all your administrative computing requirements to a computer services company.

D1

See the tapescript D1 above. The missing words are in **bold**.

D2

It *is* costing a lot of money.

We are *not* recommending any major changes.

The company sees *no* need for change.

We *do* see a need for change.

Personnel *did* know about it before.

I *do* think it's very expensive.

What we're suggesting are cuts in production.

What they propose is a major reorganisation.

What is needed is more investment not cuts in investment.

We need to reduce production costs, and we also need to reduce packaging costs.

D3.1

As we've seen ☐ we do have serious staff problems in our international loans department. ☐ So ☐ what I'm proposing ☐ is to recruit two full-time staff ☐ What are the benefits? ☐ First ☐ it will improve morale in the department ☐ Second ☐ it'll produce a more stable team. ☐ Last but not least ☐ it will give our staff more time for customer contact.

D3.1

See the tapescript D3.1 above. The pauses are marked ☐.

D3.2 Model version

a. There's *no* need to change the date of the product launch.

b. We can keep our sales and administration departments separate, but we *do* need to have them in one location.

c. Maintaining a separate research centre in Milan is *not* the most effective solution.

d. What I propose is to relocate all research and development to our factory in Frankfurt.

e. Building the plant in Spain has clear advantages. It will give us a foothold in Spain, it will give us access to a skilled workforce, and last but not least, it will give us a new factory, and all at a relatively low cost.

Referring to visuals

A Preparation

A good presentation which includes visuals will be much more effective than one without. Visuals help to:

- focus the attention of your audience
- reinforce your main ideas
- illustrate points which are hard to visualise
- involve and motivate the audience

It is most important to introduce and integrate your visuals smoothly.

Look at the two pairs of visuals below and say which of each pair is more effective. List your reasons, then check with the comments in the key.

1.

ARGUMENTS TO SUPPORT LONDON CAMPAIGN TO STAGE THE OLYMPIC GAMES IN THE YEAR 2000

- London has a strong tradition for hosting the Olympic games – already done so in 1908 and 1948.
- There are many very well known sporting venues in the city, e.g. Wembley, Wimbledon, the Royal Albert Hall and Alexandra Palace, as well as major football stadiums.
- The city has planned many new sporting facilities.
- If London is the centre for the 2000 Olympic games it will be an excellent public relations and marketing opportunity.

2.

WHY LONDON SHOULD STAGE THE 2000 OLYMPICS

- Strong Olympic tradition

- Many existing world famous sporting venues

- Many new sports facilities planned

- Excellent promotion for the capital

3.

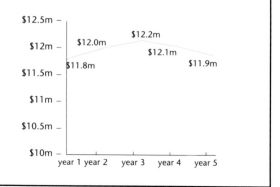

Trading Profits over
5 year period

Trading Profits in
$ millions

4.

Trading Profits
over 5 years

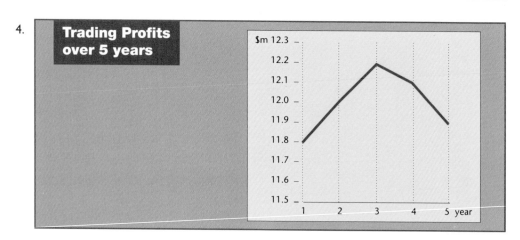

Check your answers in the key A

B What to say – Preparing the audience for a visual

B1 Focus

A large American electronics company, Switch Electronics, has operations all over the world. The company already has a European plant in France but is planning to set up in another EC country.

A member of the Human Resources Department has prepared a presentation about conditions concerning maternity leave, child benefit and other benefits in France compared to other EC countries.

Context   A company meeting.

Audience   Other staff in Human Resources at Switch Electronics.

Purpose   To brief his colleagues on the different maternity benefits in the EC countries where they are considering setting up the new plant.

The presenter has prepared a number of different slides to support his presentation.

Listen to tape B1. You will hear the presenter introduce his first two slides.

Notice how he draws the audience's attention to each slide before he gives any detailed comments on it.

As you listen, complete the missing words in the extract, then read the notes on the right.

Extract 1

.... , ... the position for maternity leave in France and in Switch Electronics.

Prepares the audience for the visual below

MATERNITY LEAVE	
FRANCE	SWITCH ELECTRONICS
....	....
16 weeks	16 weeks
6 weeks before birth	6 weeks before birth
10 weeks after birth	10 weeks after birth
Salary at 84%	Salary at 100%

Extract 2

The .... the slide .... how much maternity leave women can expect in France .... , and in Switch Electronics ....

States the purpose of the visual

Extract 3

.... the .... the slide you .... what the situation is for salary entitlement.

Expands on the purpose of the visual

Extract 4

Now, ... to the next slide, which is .... slide on child benefit. This slide gives details about child benefit in the UK.

Prepares the audience for the next visual

Check your answers in the key **BI**

B2 Summary

Preparing the audience for a visual

- Integrate your visuals into the presentation by preparing the audience for what they are going to see.
  This has two major benefits:
  - the audience is alert and ready.
  - you have extra time to position your visual correctly.

- Here are some useful expressions:
  Now, let's look at the position for …
  Now, I'll show you the …
  For … the situation is very different.
  Let's move on now and look at the figures for …
  The next slide shows …
  If we now turn to the …

- Explain what the visual shows. This helps to focus attention and avoid misunderstandings.
  This chart compares benefits in two countries …
  The upper part of the slide gives information about …
  You can see here the development over the past year.

B3 Tasks

1. All the phrases below can be used to prepare the audience for a visual, but the words are not in the correct order.
Put them in the correct order following the example.

Phrases for preparing for a visual	
a. now/show/another/I'll/slide/you ..	*Now I'll show you another slide …*
b. the/to/when/turn/we …	
c. chart/shows/the/next …	
d. turning/to/now …	
e. slide/next/the/let's/on/move/to	

Check your answers in the key **B3.1**

2. Presenters used the statements below to introduce five different visuals. But the words they used to prepare the audience for each visual are missing. Complete the statements using the phrases from B3.1.

Follow the example.

Statements

Visual 1

PRESENTER: … and we'll be looking at those figures later. **a.** *Let's move on to the next slide* . This shows you the position at the end of January.

Visual 2

… and sales didn't really move at all in this last quarter. So, overall, the performance in this sector has not been good. **b.** .... , which gives us some information about the competition.

Visual 3

c. .... a marked improvement in home sales compared to last year. This improved performance is due in part to lower interest rates…

Visual 4

… so, as we've seen, this group has not responded well to treatment. However, **d.** .... male patients we can see a more positive result.

Visual 5

e. .... the situation in the USA, which is by far our biggest market.

Check your answers in the key **B3.2**

3. Now listen to tape B3.3. You will hear the presenters introduce each of the visuals.

4. During the presentation about maternity leave and child benefit the presenter also includes the following three visuals.

Slide 2

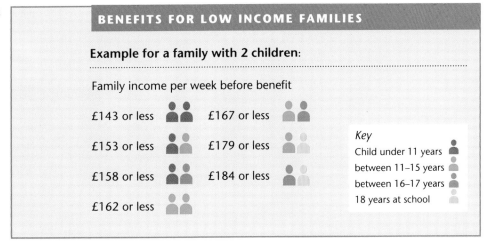

CHILD BENEFIT (UK)

| ELDEST CHILD | £8.25 per week |
| EACH OTHER CHILD | £7.25 per week |

Have you just arrived from abroad?

Benefits immediately for:
EC members staying for more than 6 months

Slide 3

BENEFITS FOR LOW INCOME FAMILIES

Example for a family with 2 children:

Family income per week before benefit

£143 or less   £167 or less

£153 or less   £179 or less

£158 or less   £184 or less

£162 or less

Key
Child under 11 years
between 11–15 years
between 16–17 years
18 years at school

Slide 4

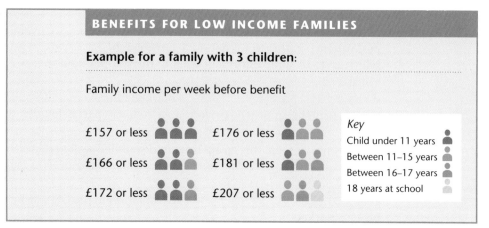

Listen to tape B3.4

You will hear the presenter comment on each of the slides. (For slide 1 see B1.)
Complete each of the presenter's commentaries by making a statement which will prepare the audience for the next slide.

You will then hear a model version.

C How to organise the information – Summarising visual information

C1 Focus

Listen to tape C1. You will hear another extract from the presentation about maternity benefits.

In this extract the presenter comments on the slide below which compares conditions in other EC countries.

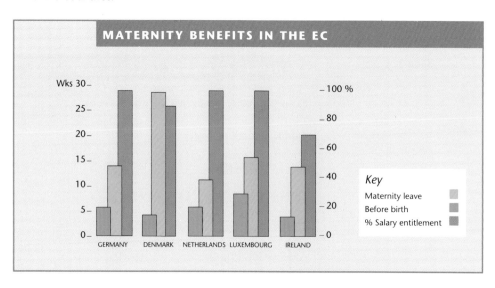

Notice how, in his commentary, the presenter does not repeat everything on the slide. Instead, he draws attention to particular features of the visual, repeats key facts, but in his own words, and adds new information. In other words he 'bounces off' the visual.

As you listen, complete the missing words in the extract. Then read the notes on the right.

Extract	Notes
.... , there are some major differences in these countries.	*Focusses on his first point of comparison*
.... all are members of the common market, and yet Denmark has nearly	*Restates facts on the visual*
.... maternity leave	
.... here.	
.... there is little consistency in the amount of time taken before and after the birth.	*Focusses on second point of comparison*
The .... , in fact, is from .... to .... weeks before the birth.	*Restates facts on the visual*
The .... offered for comparison equally shows no consistency,	*Focusses on third point of comparison*
.... of the countries offering a full 100 per cent.	*Restates facts on the visual*
It .... also .... , although	*Adds new information*
the	
.... , other members of the community including France and Spain offer less than 100 per cent salary during maternity leave.	

Check your answers in the key **C1**

C2 Summary

Commenting on visuals

In the commentaries which accompany your visuals:
- Keep headlines and other information on the visual to a minimum.
- Only point out the key features or information which you want your audience to focus on.
- Briefly restate key facts from the visual rather than reading the information on the visual word for word. This will help to reinforce the information for the audience.
- Add other *related* information not on the visual in order to make further points.
- Give interpretations and/or any comments.

C3 Tasks

1. The headline below is from another visual for the presentation about maternity benefits. It is too long. Prepare a shorter headline.

> **SOME COMPARISONS BETWEEN THE RIGHTS OF WORKING WOMEN IN FRANCE, ITALY AND GREECE WITH REFERENCE TO MATERNITY LEAVE AND SALARY DURING MATERNITY LEAVE**

Check your answers in the key   C3.1

2. The chart below is the main part of the visual for C3.1.

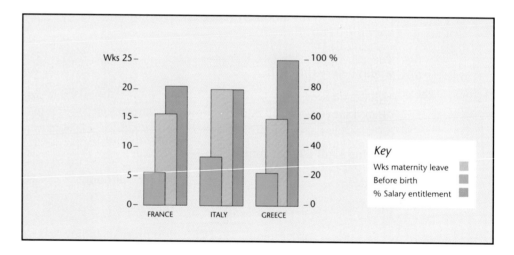

Complete the commentary below for this visual by adding the related information about a non-EC country, Finland. The information is in the box below.

> *Commentary*
>
> … as you can see, Italy has the best situation here, even though the actual percentage paid on salary is not quite as high. Of course, these figures are for countries which are members of the community. ....

> **Maternity leave in Finland**
>
> Mother: 5 weeks before the birth
>   15 weeks after the birth
>
> Father: 6–12 days

Check your answers in the key   C3.2

3. Prepare a short commentary for the graph below. Follow the instructions below.

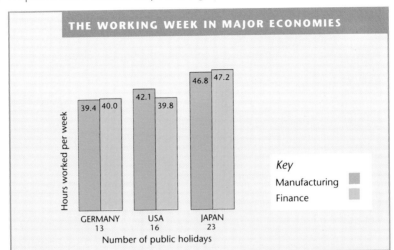

THE WORKING WEEK IN MAJOR ECONOMIES

Hours worked per week

39.4 | 40.0 | 42.1 | 39.8 | 46.8 | 47.2

GERMANY 13 | USA 16 | JAPAN 23

Number of public holidays

Key
Manufacturing
Finance

Instructions

a. Focus on the first point of comparison – how much longer people work in Japan than in Germany or the USA.

b. Restate facts from the visual – in the manufacturing sector the average German worker works 39.4 hours per week. Japanese worker works 46.8 hours.

c. Focus on the second point of comparison – big differences in the financial sector.

d. Focus on the third point of comparison – the fact that Japan has the highest number of public holidays, 23 in Japan as compared to 13 in Germany and 16 in the USA.

e. Add a comment – possible explanation for why the Japanese work such long hours.

Now listen to a version of the commentary on tape C3.3.

D How to create interest – Focussing your audience's attention

... AND SO ON BLAH BLAH AND SUCH AND SUCH BLAH BLAH AND HERE'S ANOTHER INTERESTING POINT BLAH BLAH...

D1 Focus

Listen to tape D1. You will hear six short extracts from different presentations.

In each extract the presenter draws the audience's attention to a particular feature of the visual. Listen to each extract and complete the phrases. Then read the notes below.

Extract 1

Now, we come to our soft drinks division. Results in this sector have been generally

satisfactory this year, and in particular ....

.... the steady growth in the last quarter.

Notice that this is quite a formal expression.

Extract 2

Let's take a look at the effect on the oil price in the early stages of the war.

.... , the oil price held steady right the way through this period.

Notice that the presenter identifies with the audience by the use of *we*.

Extract 3

Seasonality does not affect all products, but there is one range of our products

where its effect is noticeable. In the next slide .... the way in which the seasonal variation is so marked in sales of soft drinks.

Notice that this has the form of an instruction, but it does not sound formal because of the presenter's intonation.

Extract 4

We then found that our running costs at our sales offices in Germany and France varied by as much as 20 per cent, and that there was also a difference between costs in Britain and Germany. This variation in the running costs for our different

sales offices is ....

Notice that the speaker uses an adjective to arouse interest.

Extract 5

As you know, we moved into the Japanese market three years ago, at a time when we were hearing a lot of advice about not making that move. Well, I have some

recent figures which I'd like you to look at. .... is ....

.... here, is just how quickly our market share in Japan has increased.

Notice that the presenter catches her audience's attention by starting her sentence with *what*.

Extract 6

Yesterday when we held our meeting with the regional sales directors, we looked at the effect of discounting in the supermarkets. The situation appears to be that,

after some initial success, sales have once again dropped off. The ....
point is that the trend is not new. In fact, three years ago when we were ...

Notice that the presenter again uses an adjective to arouse interest

Check your answers in the key **D1**

D2 Summary

Focussing your audience's attention

- Here are some useful expressions to focus your audience's attention on particular features on a visual.

  You can see the …

  As you /we can see …

  What is interesting/important is …

  And more formally:

  I'd like to draw your attention to …

  Notice / Observe the …

  It is important/interesting to notice that …

- Another way to focus attention on a particular feature of a visual is to use a *dramatic* piece of vocabulary, e.g.

  The position of this equipment is **extremely dangerous**

  This sudden rise in prices was **quite unexpected.**

  (See extracts 4, 5 and 6 in D1 above.)

Dramatic vocabulary

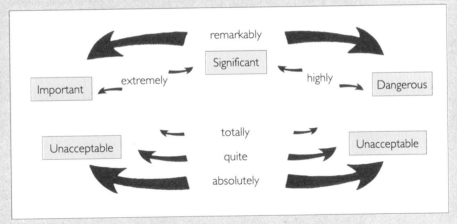

D3 Tasks

1. Draw your audience's attention to the information in the charts below, using expressions from the summary.

Chart 1

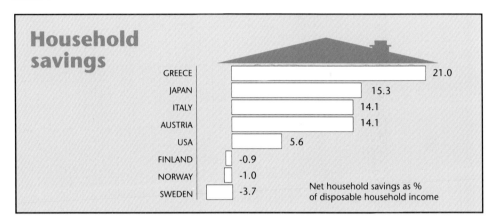

Note: The chart is part of a formal presentation. Draw attention to:

a. The high proportion of savings in Greece.

I'd like to draw your attention to the very high level of savings in Greece.

b. The negative savings in the Nordic countries.

c. The similar levels of savings in Italy and Austria.

Chart 2

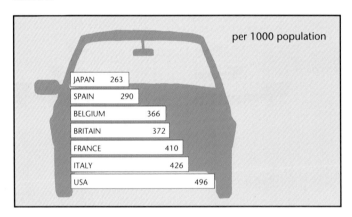

Note: This chart is part of an informal presentation.

d. Spain as potentially one of the best markets in Europe.

You can see that Spain is potentially one of the best markets for cars in Europe.

e. The number of cars in the USA – perhaps not really unexpected.

f. The relatively low number of cars in Japan considering its development.

Check your answers in the key **D3.1**

2. The chart below is from a presentation surveying attitudes to national institutions in different EC countries.

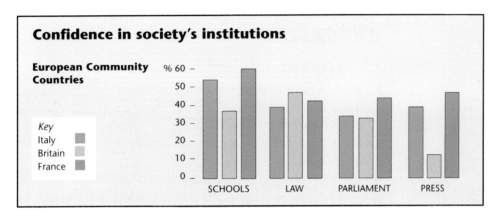

Decide what the presenter would say to draw attention to the following facts in the chart. Use dramatic vocabulary from the D2 summary.

a. The fact that all three countries have rather low confidence in the law, which the presenter thinks is important.

Example

It is extremely worrying that all three countries have such low confidence in their legal institutions / the law.

b. The low level of confidence in schools in the UK, which the presenter finds worrying.

c. The fact that the UK has such low confidence in the press, which the presenter didn't expect.

d. The high level of confidence of the French in their schools, which the presenter thinks is significant.

Check your answers in the key **D3.2**

E Activities

1. Prepare a visual on a work-related topic, or use a visual from a presentation you have already given yourself. Use the framework below to help you plan your commentary.

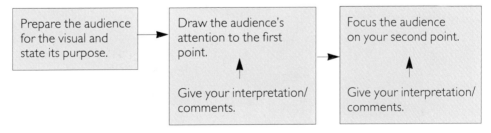

CHECKLIST

Yes/No

- Is there the right amount of information on the visual?
- Does the layout help the audience to understand
  the point of the visual?
- Is the lettering clear and easy to read?
- Do the colours you've used really work?
- Are there any spelling or grammatical mistakes?

Prepare verbal commentaries for the three visuals and decide how to integrate them smoothly into your presentation.

Now give the presentation. If possible, record yourself.

CHECKLIST

Yes/No

- Did you prepare the audience by telling them what
  the visual was about in advance?
- Did you direct the audience's attention to the main
  points on the visual?
- Did you rephrase the main information
  you wanted the audience to focus on?
- Did you analyse and comment on the information?

Answer key

A Preparation

Comments

Visual 2

This is better laid out. The other visual has much too much detail on it.

Visual 4

The use of colour is much better. The colouring on the other graph makes it difficult to read. The use of a larger scale makes the trend clearer visually.

B What to say

B.1

Extract 1

PRESENTER: **Now, let's look at** the position for maternity leave in France and in Switch Electronics.

Extract 2

PRESENTER: The **top half of** the slide **tells you** how much maternity leave women can expect in France **in general**, and in Switch Electronics **in particular**.

Extract 3

PRESENTER: **In** the **lower part of** the slide you **can see** what the situation is for salary entitlement.

Extract 4

PRESENTER: Now, **let's move on** to the next slide, which is **our first** slide on child benefit. This slide gives details about child benefit in the UK.

B1

See tapescript B1 above. The missing words are in **bold**.

B3.1

a. Now I'll show you another slide …

b. When we turn to the …

c. The next chart shows …

d. Now turning to …

e. Let's move on to the next slide.

B3.2

a. Let's move on to the next slide

b. Now I'll show you another slide

c. The next chart shows

d. When we turn to the

e. Now turning to

B3.3

Visual 1

PRESENTER: … and we'll be looking at those figures later. **Let's move on to the next slide.** This shows you the position at the end of January.

Visual 2

PRESENTER: … and sales didn't really move at all in this last quarter. So, overall, the performance in this sector has not been good. **Now I'll show you another slide**, which gives us some information about the competition.

Visual 3

PRESENTER: **The next chart shows** a marked improvement in home sales compared to last year. This improved performance is due in part to lower interest rates …

Visual 4

PRESENTER: … so, as we've seen, this group has not responded well to treatment. However, **when we turn to the** male patients we can see a more positive result.

Visual 5

PRESENTER: **Now turning to** the situation in the USA, which is by far our biggest market.

B3.4

Presenter	So, we've seen that for maternity leave entitlement the parents of children working for Switch Electronics seem to have a slightly better deal than is generally the case in France.
Your statement	....
Model version	**Now I'd like to move on to the next chart which gives details about child benefit in the UK.**

Presenter	A family receives £8.25 for the eldest qualifying child, and £7.25 for each other child. Note also the benefits to residents from outside the UK.
Your statement	....
Model version	**My next chart will look at benefits for families on lower incomes.**
Presenter	The system of additional benefit, known as family credit, can be applied for for children up to the age of fifteen. Well, those are the figures for a family with two children.
Your statement	....
Model version	**Now, let's look at the figures for a family with three children.**

C How to organise the information

C1 🎧

PRESENTER: **As you can see**, there are some major differences in these countries. **Remember that** all are members of the common market, and yet Denmark has nearly **twice as much** maternity leave **as any other country** here.

Notice also that there is little consistency in the amount of time taken before and after the birth.

The **range**, in fact, is from **four** to **eight** weeks before the birth.

The **third set of figures** offered for comparison equally shows no consistency, **with only three** of the countries offering a full 100 per cent.

It **is** also **interesting that**, although the **figures aren't actually given here**, other members of the community including France and Spain offer less than 100 per cent salary during maternity leave.

C1

See tapescript C1 above. The missing words are in **bold**.

C3.1 Model version

Maternity leave in the EC

or

Maternity benefit and salary in the EC

C3.2 Model version

It is interesting to compare these figures with a non-EC member, Finland. As in Italy, the mother receives 20 weeks but in addition, the father is also paid for up to 12 working days.

C3.3 🎧 Model version

PRESENTER: It's interesting to see just how much longer working hours are in Japan. All three countries are major economic powers, and yet, in the manufacturing sector, the average German worker spends about seven hours less at work than his Japanese counterpart. When we turn to the financial sector we can see that there are also great differences, with the Japanese working on average a 47.2 hour week. That's over 7 hours more than either his or her US and German counterpart works in this sector.

It's also very interesting that Japan has the highest number of public holidays, with seven days more than the USA and 10 days more than Germany.

Perhaps this explains why the Japanese work such long hours.

D How to create interest

D1 🎧

Extract 1

PRESENTER: Now we come to our soft drinks division. Results in this sector have been generally satisfactory this year, and in particular **I'd like to draw your attention to** the steady growth in the last quarter.

Extract 2

PRESENTER: Let's take a look at the effect on the oil price in the early stages of the war. **As we can see**, the oil price held steady right the way through this period.

Extract 3

PRESENTER: Seasonality does not affect all products, but there is one range of our products where its effect is noticeable. In the next slide **notice** the way in which the seasonal variation is so marked in sales of soft drinks.

Extract 4

PRESENTER: We then found that our running costs at our sales offices in Germany and France varied by as much as 20 per cent, and that there was also a difference between costs in Britain and Germany. This variation in the running costs for our different sales offices is **extremely surprising**.

Extract 5

PRESENTER: As you know, we moved into the Japanese market three years ago, at a time when we were hearing a lot of advice about not making that move. Well, I have some recent figures which I'd like you to look at. **What** is **particularly interesting** here, is just how quickly our market share in Japan has increased.

Extract 6

PRESENTER: Yesterday when we held our meeting with the regional sales directors, we looked at the effect of discounting in the supermarkets. The situation appears to be that, after some initial success, sales have once again dropped off. The **worrying** point is that the trend is not new. In fact, three years ago when we were…

D1

See tapescript D1 above. The missing words are in **bold**.

D3.1 Model version

b. It is interesting to notice the level of saving in the Nordic countries.

c. Notice / observe how similar levels of savings are in Italy and Austria.

e. As you can see, the USA has the highest number of cars which is, perhaps, not really unexpected.

f. What is interesting is how few cars there are in Japan, especially when you consider how developed it is.

D3.2 Model version

b. The low level of confidence in British schools is extremely/particularly worrying.

c. The low level of confidence in the press in the UK is quite/very unexpected.

d. The high level of confidence in the French school-system is highly/extremely significant.

or

It is very significant/extremely significant that the French have such a high level of confidence in their schools.

Concluding the presentation

A   *Preparation*

B   *What to say*   Recommendations and calls for action

C   *How to organise the information*   Summaries, conclusions and closing courtesies

D   *How to create interest*   Giving your message more impact

E   *Activities*

A Preparation

Without a good conclusion a presentation is not complete. One way to end a presentation is to summarise briefly your main arguments and draw conclusions for the audience.

Listen to tape A1.

You will hear the conclusions to four presentations.

Complete the statements below.

Presentation 1 – The consolidation of European computing at Marcon chemicals.
a. The presenter wants the audience to ....

Presentation 2 – Review of the performance of Aqua-Sparkle.
b. The presenter wants the audience to go away from the presentation with a clear idea about ....
c. He also wants his audience to ....

Presentation 3 – Selection and orientation procedures for employees due to go on overseas assignments.

d. The presenter wants her audience to go away from the presentation with a clear idea about ....

Presentation 4 – An office automation proposal.

e. The presenter wants the audience to ....

Check your answers in the key **A1**

B *What to say – Recommendations and calls for action*

B1 Focus

The conclusion of a persuasive presentation often includes recommendations or a call for action.

Listen to tape B1.

You will hear the conclusions from the two persuasive presentations in A1 again. In both conclusions the presenters recommend a course of action. Notice how the presenters make their recommendations.

Complete the missing words in each extract and read the notes on the right.

Presentation – Consolidation of European computing at Marcon Chemicals

Extract	Notes

... there is and will be a major need for new computer

applications. So, ...   *First recommendation*

.... leave them as they are ...

... and is creating problems of duplication. ....   *Second recommendation*

therefore .... a thorough reorganisation ...

... and the time factor. So, the ....   *Final recommendation*

.... for more detailed

...................., ... sub-contract all
administrative computing ...

Presentation – An office automation proposal

Extract

So, in conclusion, I ....   *Call for action*

.... the new office automation scheme

....

And, ... have a   *Proposal for next step*

decision ....

the month, ... to work out

a detailed plan .... December, which

means .... announce the new project

.... January.

Check your answers in the key **B I**

B2 Summary

Recommendations and calls for action

- A persuasive presentation will often include recommendations and/or a call for action from the audience.

- At this stage the following vocabulary is often useful.

Recommendation	*Recommend*
Proposal	*Propose*
Suggestion	*Suggest*

Notice how they are used:

My suggestion *Our proposal* *The recommendation*	*would be/is to set up a project group.*
We recommend *I'd like to suggest* *I propose*	*setting up a project group.*
We suggest *I recommend* *We propose*	*you set up a project group.*

B3 Tasks

1. Below you will find four recommendations from different presentations. Complete each recommendation by matching information from columns **A** and **B**.
Follow the example.

A	B
a. We propose	i. is to centralize all our R and D in Brussels.
b. The recommendations of this study	ii investing in new production facilities.
c. The solution we favour	iii a major sales push in the Japanese market.
d. We strongly urge you to consider	iv. are to sub-contract all training to outside suppliers.

Check your answers in the key **B3.1**

2. If the recommendations in the last exercises are accepted the presenters also propose the following actions.

Complete the presenters' recommendations. Again combine information from columns **A** and **B**.

Follow the example.

A	B
a. But, if we really want to target the Japanese market,	i. we could carry out a detailed study of training organisations by the beginning of November.
b. If we could have your decision before the end of the month,	ii you'll need to carry out a more detailed study of the manpower implications.
c. But before any final decision is taken about closing our other R and D facilities,	iii we should have all our literature in Japanese.
d. If you decide to go ahead with the investment,	iv. you'll need to look at different ways of raising the money.

Check your answers in the key `B3.2`

C How to organise the information – *Summaries, conclusions and closing courtesies*

C1 Focus

Listen to tape C1.

You will then hear the conclusion to presentation one again.

Notice how the presenter builds up the conclusion. First she reviews the main findings of the study and gives her conclusions, then she brings the presentation to an end.

Notice the sentences and phrases the presenter uses as she builds up her conclusion.

Complete the missing words in the extract. Then read the notes on the right.

Extract	Notes
At this stage	*Introduces her summary*
.... the main findings of the study.	
.... , the manufacturing data centres.	*Reviews the situation for manufacturing data centres*
Given the rapid growth in business in your plants...	
.... , our recommendation is to leave them as they are.	*Makes recommendation*
... Their organisation is not cost-effective, and is creating problems of duplication.	*Reviews situation for administrative data centres,*
We .... recommend a thorough reorganisation.	*and makes recommendation*
We've looked at three options. .... , to set up three regional data centres...	*Reviews options*
.... option, to expand one of the existing regional data centres ...	

.... , ... which we strongly
recommend for more detailed consideration, is to sub-
contract all administrative computing to an outside supplier...

Then makes final recommendation

.... detailed cost breakdowns for the three

options, ...

Refers audience to documentation

.... now.

And, of course, ...

.... any ....

Asks for questions

.... all ....

Thanks the audience

....

Check your answers in the key `C1`

C2 Summary

Building up a conclusion

A good conclusion will contain some or all of the following stages.

* A summary
  Often a summary is needed before you give your final conclusions.
  Review or restate your key points from the introduction and main body of the
  presentation. This helps to reinforce them for your audience.
  So, to summarise/sum up ...
  At this stage I'd like to go over/run through ...
  So, as we've seen in this presentation today, ...
  As I've explained, ...

* Conclusions
  This will often take the form of:
    a recommendation or call for action
    a challenge
    a dynamic concluding statement to reinforce your message

* Support documentation
  At this stage of your presentation it would be appropriate to distribute support
  documents, folders, cost breakdown, handouts, calculations or copies of OHP
  transparencies.
  I've a detailed cost breakdown, which I'll be passing/handing round now.
  In the folder which I'll be distributing you'll find copies of the ...

* Closing formalities.
  I'd be happy to answer any questions.
  If you have any questions, I'd be pleased to answer them.
  I would welcome any comments/suggestions.
  Thank you for your attention.

C3 Tasks

1. The statements below are from the conclusion for a presentation reviewing the performance of chocolate products, but they are not in a logical order.

Put the statements in a logical order.

Follow the example.

Statements

a. Clearly, if we are to improve our performance in this sector, action must be taken in the coming year.

b. So, in conclusion. I would ask you to give serious consideration to these measures.

c. Thank you for your attention, and if you have any questions I'd be happy to answer them.

d. But, faced with strong competition, the performance of our remaining sector, bags of chocolates, is very disappointing.

e. And, I'm confident that the measures which I've outlined today will do just that.

START ➔ f. So, as we've seen, the product sectors, boxes and blocks have performed well. **(1)**

Check your answers in the key **C3.1**

2. The staff in the foreign loans department in the UK subsidiary of an American bank are having to work considerable amounts of overtime.

The Department Manager has looked at two options for solving the problem, to hire

i. temporary staff

ii. permanent staff

The notes below are his conclusion for a presentation about this problem.

Study the presentation plan.

Summary

Clear problem in the department
      staff overworked and making mistakes
      deterioration in customer service

Case against 1st solution – hire temporary staff
      will compound the problem by creating need for:
      extra training
      constant supervision of temporary staff

Conclusion recommend 2nd solution – hire more permanent staff
      solve overtime problem
      opportunity to create effective team of specialists

Distribute cost breakdown for two options

Listen to tape C3.2.

You will hear six instructions asking you to develop the conclusion for this presentation. Make your response after each instruction.

You will then hear a model version.

Example

Instruction 1	Introduce your summary.
Your response	....
Model version	**So, just to summarise. It's clear we have a serious problem in the department.**

D How to create interest – Giving your message more impact

D1 Focus

Listen to tape D1. You will hear extracts from the four conclusions in A1.

Notice how the presenters emphasise key ideas in their conclusion. They do this by their choice of vocabulary, and by stressing certain words.

As you listen complete the missing words in the extracts.

Extract 1

Consolidation of Marcon's European computing

So, the option which we .... recommend for more detailed consideration is to sub-contract .... administrative computing to an outside supplier of computer services.

Extract 2

Performance of Aqua-Sparkle

As you've seen, the brand is performing .... in this sector, and some customers have .... decided to delist the brand because it is priced

....

Extract 3

Performance of Aqua-Sparkle

For the reasons I've explained, discounting the brand is not an option if we .... want to maintain our premium positioning. So we're looking for other ways to .... our lemonade .... of the Independent Grocers.

Extract 4

New selection and orientation procedures

Therefore, we've changed the procedures for selection and orientation, and have managed to .... our success rate to 90 per cent which, ..., is a .... satisfactory level.

Check your answers in the key **D1**

D2 Summary

Giving your message more impact

- It is important to make your conclusions as forceful and as memorable as possible.
- Notice how the words in **bold** give more emphasis to the points.

*It's priced **so** high customers are delisting the brand.*

*If we **really** want to reach our target, we need a higher budget.*

*Given the **very/extremely** high costs, we should look for another solution.*

*The quality **just** isn't high enough.*

*The timescale is **far too** ambitious.*

*We **really** feel/think this is the best way to to proceed.*

*We **strongly** recommend the first option.*

*I wish to make it **quite** clear that this is **only** a temporary solution.*

D3 Tasks

1. Make the sentences below sound stronger.
Follow the example.

a. As we've seen, the budget is ...*really* ... *far* ... *too* ... low.

b. Our costs are .... high we .... aren't competitive any more.

c. Given the .... high costs of a central office, we .... recommend relocating your administrative functions out of London.

d. If you .... want to create an effective sales team, you need to hire .... qualified staff.

e. It's .... clear that the system .... isn't working.

Check your answers in the key **D3.1**

2. Listen to tape D3.2. You will hear the conclusion from the presentation about new selection and orientation procedures for overseas assignees.

Notice how the presenter slows down and pauses as she gives her conclusion. She does this to give more impact to what she is saying, and to give her audience time to think about the message.

Script

I am aware that some of you may feel that the costs and the time we've invested in preparing overseas assignees for their new contracts ☐ are much higher ☐ than many companies would wish to bear ☐ However ☐ I would like you to consider also the cost of replacing someone who returns early from a contract ☐ not only the financial costs but ☐ more importantly ☐ the costs to the company's reputation ☐ And I'm sure that if you consider those costs ☐ you will feel that the time and the money we've spent in implementing these new methods ☐ and achieving the improved success rate ☐ are well justified.

---

3. The two extracts below are from the conclusions from two different presentations.

Mark where you think the presenters will pause to give more impact to what they are saying.

> *Extract 1*
>
> Our results for this year are satisfactory but we feel there's still room for improvement. The question is are we going to sit back and enjoy the success we've achieved so far, or press on to even better achievements?
>
> *Extract 2*
>
> We've allowed just four months to prepare detailed plans for the new system. We realise it's an ambitious timescale but we're confident it can be achieved.

Now listen to tape D3.3. You will hear the two extracts.

4. The conclusion below is from the presentation about the staffing problem in the foreign loans department of the UK bank.

How would you change it to make it more powerful and memorable?
Think about words you can change or add, and where you would pause to give more impact to what you are saying.

If possible record your version.

> *Script*
>
> I recommend the second option, which is to hire more permanent staff. If we hire staff on a permanent basis we can solve the overtime problem. And, we will also be able to create a team of specialists. This team will be able to cope with the increasing work load, and offer our customers a higher quality of service.

Now listen to tape D3.4. You will hear a model version of the conclusion.

E Activities

I. Choose one of the topics below for a presentation.

> ~ *A project update*   ~ *A change in a procedure*
> ~ *A performance review*   ~ *A new product/system.*

a. Complete the two statements about your presentation.
   The purpose of this presentation is ....
   At the end of the presentation I want my audience to ....
b. Brainstorm your key points and list them in note form.
c. Plan a conclusion for the presentation. Use one of the frameworks to help you organise your ideas.

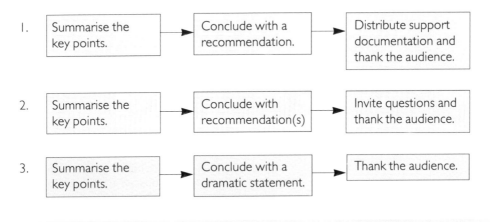

1. Summarise the key points. → Conclude with a recommendation. → Distribute support documentation and thank the audience.

2. Summarise the key points. → Conclude with recommendation(s) → Invite questions and thank the audience.

3. Summarise the key points. → Conclude with a dramatic statement. → Thank the audience.

CHECKLIST

	Yes/No	Example
■ Did you include a clear summary of the main points?		
■ Was it clear for the audience what message you wanted them to take away?		
■ Was it clear what you wanted the audience to do?		
■ Did you manage to create an impact with your ending?		

Answer key

A Preparation

AI

a. Consider her proposal for the administrative data centres i.e. sub-contract all administrative data processing to an outside supplier.

b. How Aqua-Sparkle has performed in the lemonade market.

c. Suggest ways to improve its performance in the Independent Grocers sector.

d. The importance of selection and orientation procedures when sending personnel to work abroad.

e. Give their decision about the proposed office automation scheme before the end of the month.

AI

Presentation 1

PRESENTER: At this stage I'd like to summarise the main findings of the study. First, the manufacturing data centres. Given the rapid growth in business in your plants, there is and will be a major need for new computer applications. So our recommendation is to leave them as they are.

However, with the administrative data centres we have a very different situation. Their organisation is not cost-effective, and is creating problems of duplication. We therefore recommend a thorough reorganisation.

We've looked at three options. First, to set up three regional data centres, but this represents only a partial solution to the problem of duplication and, as we've seen, is really not viable.

The second option, to expand one of the existing regional data centres in Bristol, Barcelona or Frankfurt, would achieve an efficient use of our resources, but there are physical problems such as lack of space, and the time factor.

So, the option which we strongly recommend for more detailed consideration, is to sub-contract all administrative computing to an outside supplier of computer services.

I've detailed cost breakdowns for the three options, which I'll be passing round now. And, of course, I'll be pleased to answer any questions.

Thank you all for your attention.

Presentation 2

PRESENTER: To summarise. Firstly, the overall performance of the lemonade category has not been good, due, as I've explained, to general economic factors.

Secondly, sales of Aqua-Sparkle are down but, like other premium brands, it has performed much better in the market than the lower priced brands.

Thirdly, the outlook for the lemonade category is not bright. However, because of its premium positioning we can expect to see Aqua-Sparkle continuing to perform better in the market than many of its competitors.

Fourthly, and this brings me to the main area of concern, there's the problem we've identified in the Independent Grocers sector. As you've seen, the brand is performing badly in this sector, and some customers have actually decided to delist the brand because it's priced so high. For the reasons I've explained, discounting the brand is not an option if we really want to maintain our premium positioning. So, we're looking for other ways to bring our lemonade back onto the shelves of the Independent Grocers, and I would welcome your suggestions.

Thank you for your attention.

Presentation 3

PRESENTER: So, as we've seen today, the study we carried out indicated two main reasons for the early return of staff from overseas contracts – inadequate preparation for living and working in a strange culture and environment, and the poor selection procedures.

Therefore, we've changed the procedures for selection and orientation, and have managed to boost our success rate to 90 per cent, which

I'm sure you will agree is a very satisfactory level. I am aware that some of you may feel that the costs and the time we've invested in preparing overseas assignees for their new contracts are much higher than many companies would wish to bear. However, I would like you to consider also the cost of replacing someone who returns early from a contract, not only the financial costs but, more importantly, the costs to the company's reputation. And I'm sure that if you consider those costs, you will feel that the time and the money we've spent in implementing these new procedures and achieving the improved success rate are well justified.

Thank you for your attention, and if there are any questions, I'd be happy to answer them. Thank you.

Presentation 4

PRESENTER: So, in conclusion, I would like you to give the new office automation scheme your serious consideration. And, if we can have a decision by the end of the month, we'll be able to work out a detailed plan by mid-December, which means we can announce the new project in early January.

B *What to say*

B1

Presentation – European computing

So, **our recommendation is to** leave them as they are.
We therefore **recommend** a thorough reorganisation.
So, the **option which we strongly recommend** for more detailed **consideration is to** sub-contract all administrative computing…

Presentation – Office automation

So, in conclusion, I **would like you to give** the new office automation scheme **your serious consideration**.
And, **if we can** have a decision **before the end of** the month, **we'll be able** to work out a detailed plan **by mid**-December, which means **we can** announce the project **in early** January.

B1 🖭

Refer to tape A1, presentations 1 and 4 for the full tapescript.

B3.1

a. iii   b. iv   c. i   d. ii
In a ii ⎫
    d iii ⎬   is gramatically possible

B3.2

a. iii   b. i   c. ii   d. iv

C *How to organise the information*

C1

I'd like to summarise …

First …

So …

… therefore …

First … **The second** … . **So, the option** …

I've … **which I'll be passing around** …

… I'll be pleased to answer … **questions**
Thank you … **for your attention.**

C1 🖭

Refer to A1, presentation 1 for the full tapescript.

C3.1

f. d. a. e. b. c

C3.2 🖭

Instruction 1	Introduce the summary.
Your response	…………………………………
Model version	**So, just to summarise. It's clear we have a problem in the department.**
Instruction 2	Review the problem.
Your response	…………………………………
Model version	**As we've seen, staff are overworked and are making mistakes. Another problem, customer service is deteriorating.**
Instruction 3	Review the first solution and the case against it.
Your response	…………………………………
Model version	**The first solution we've looked at is to hire temporary staff, but this will only compound the problem by creating needs for extra training and constant supervision of temporary staff.**
Instruction 4	Conclude with your recommendation.

Your response ....

Model version **So my recommendation is the second solution, which is to hire more permanent staff. Recruiting permanent staff will give us a major opportunity to create a really effective team of specialists.**

Instruction 5   Refer the audience to the handout.

Your response ....

Model version **I have a cost breakdown for the two solutions, which I'll be passing round now.**

Instruction 6   Thank the audience and invite questions.

Your response ....

Model version **Thank you for your attention, and if you have any questions, I'd be pleased to answer them.**

D How to create interest

D1 📼

Extract 1

PRESENTER: So, the option which we **strongly** recommend for more detailed consideration, is to sub-contract **all** administrative computing to an outside supplier of computer services.

Extract 2

PRESENTER: As you've seen, the brand is performing **badly** in this sector, and some customers have **actually** decided to delist the brand because it is priced **so high**.

Extract 3

PRESENTER: For the reasons I've explained, discounting the brand is not an option if we **really** want to maintain our premium positioning. So we're looking for other ways to **bring** our lemonade **back onto the shelves** of the Independent Grocers.

Extract 4

PRESENTER: Therefore, we've changed the procedures for selection and orientation, and have managed to **boost** our success rate to 90 per cent, which **I'm sure you will agree**, is a **very** satisfactory level.

D1

See tapescript D1 above. The missing words are in **bold**.

D3.1

a. really far/much too low

b. so … just/simply/really

c. extremely/very… strongly

d. really … highly

e. quite … … just …

D3.2 📼

PRESENTER: I am aware that some of you may feel that the costs and the time we've invested in preparing overseas assignees for their new contracts are much higher than many companies would wish to bear. However, I would like you to consider also the cost of replacing someone who returns early from a contract; not only the financial costs but, more importantly, the costs to the company's reputation. And I'm sure that if you consider those costs, you will feel that the time and the money we've spent in implementing these new methods and achieving the improved success rate are well justified.

D3.3 📼

PRESENTER: Our results for this year are satisfactory ☐ but we feel there's still room for improvement ☐ The question is ☐ are we going to sit back and enjoy the success we've achieved so far ☐ or press on ☐ to even better achievements?

PRESENTER: We've allowed just four months to prepare detailed plans for the new system ☐ We realise it's an ambitious timescale ☐ but we're confident it can be achieved.

Key

☐ a short pause

D3.3 📼

See the answer key above for the tapescript.

D3.4 Model version

PRESENTER: I strongly recommend the second option ☐ which is to hire more permanent staff ☐ This will not only solve the overtime problem ☐ but it will also give us the opportunity ☐ to create a really effective team of specialists ☐ who are able to cope with the increasing work load ☐ and offer our customers a higher quality of service.

D3.4 📼

See the key D3.4 above for the full tapescript.

Handling questions

A Preparation	Understanding questions
B What to say	Clarifying questions
C How to use tactics	Handling difficult or hostile questions
D How to handle information	Offering help to clarify information
E Activities	

A Preparation

Most presentations include time for questions and answers. Sometimes presenters ask for questions during the presentation, but more frequently there is a question time at the end of the presentation.

A large American company, Marcon Chemicals, has made the decision to sub-contract its European administrative computing to an outside supplier of computing services.

The Head of the Human Resources Department is presenting the manpower implications to senior managers from the different subsidiaries.

I. The questions below were asked during the presentations. Which ones were asked:
   a. because something was not clear?
   b. to raise doubts about a point?
   c. to get more information?

1
How many data centres did you say will have to close?

5
You said some staff will be transferred to our manufacturing data centres. Does that mean a big expansion in their activity?

2
I agree that sub-contracting is the best solution, but can you explain why people weren't informed about the decision straight away?

6
Isn't it the case that the decision to close down the data centres was taken months ago?

7
Could you give us some more information about how you propose to deal with retraining?

3
Isn't there a major security risk involved in sub-contracting to an outside supplier?

8
I have a question about the data centres. What will happen to them after they close down?

4
I can see big advantages in a single data centre, but is 1993 realistic?

9
I'm not really clear about the timescale for the project. Could you explain it again?

Check your answers in the key **A1**

🔲 **2.** Now listen to tape. A2. You will hear all the questions from the last exercise.

Say which questions are:

a. Hostile in tone

b. Neutral

Check your answers in the key **A2**

B What to say – Clarifying questions

B1 Focus

🔲 Listen to tape B1. You will hear extracts from the questioning phase of three different presentations. Notice how the presenters make sure they understand the questions before they give their answers.

Listen to the questions and answers. As you listen, complete the missing words in each extract. Then read the notes on the right.

Extract 1

Notes

Question

Yes, I wonder if you could say a little more about the trend for Aqua-Sparkle? Is it seasonal, or is there another explanation for the fall-off in sales in the early part of the year?

Asks for more information

Answer

Well, it is seasonal to a certain extent.

Asks for clarification before replying

.... at the January/February figures?

Extract 2

Question

Excuse me, but when you mentioned the growth in profits, did you mean to say that the company is going to have more money to invest in plant and equipment next year?

*Refers back to a point in the presentation
Then asks for clarification*

Answer

.... , do we plan to plough back profits into investments for production next year?

....?

*Rephrases question to make sure he understands
Then asks for clarification*

Extract 3

Question

Could I have another look at the slide which shows when we'll break even?

Asks to see the slide again

Answer

...., ... didn't ....

Apologises

Which slide ....?

Then asks the questioner to repeat his request

Check your answers in the key   **B1**

B2 Summary

Clarifying questions

- Before you answer any question, make sure you really understand it. Here are some useful tactics you can use.

Rephrasing the original question

So, do we plan to plough back profits …?
So, what you're asking is …
If I understand the question correctly, you would like to know …

Asking further questions to clarify the question

Are you looking at the January/February figures?
When you say … do you mean … ?

Asking for repetition

I'm sorry, I didn't hear. Which slide was it?
Sorry, could you repeat that?

B3 Tasks

1. Listen to tape B3.1.

You will hear questions and answers from the questioning phase of three different presentations. Which tactic does the presenter use to make sure he or she really understands the question?

Match each of the presenter's answers with one of the tactics.

Follow the example.

Question	Presenter's tactic
a.	i. asking for repetition
b.	ii rephrasing
c.	iii asking for clarification

Check your answers in the key **B3.1**

2. Listen to tape B3.2. You will hear four questions.

Answer each question following the instructions below. Make your response after each of the questions. You will then hear a model version.

Question	Instruction	
a.	Ask for a clarification	– which product line?
b.	Ask for a repetition	– what product number?
c.	Rephrase the question	– explanation for our confidence in fertilizers as a major growth area in the coming year.
d.	Rephrase the question	– why so optimistic about the figures for the second quarter?

C How to use tactics – Handling difficult or hostile questions

Sometimes you may have to handle difficult or hostile questions from the audience. These can be handled using a variety of tactics e.g. by delaying answering the question or evading the question altogether.

The chart below is from the presentation about the manpower implications of sub-contracting administrative computing at Marcon Chemicals. It shows the status of the 60 people who will be affected by the decision to close the data centres.

Look at the chart and think of four questions you would like to ask the presenter.

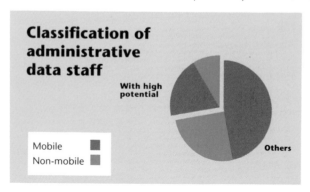

There is no key to this activity.

C1 Focus

📻 Listen to tape C1.

You will hear four extracts from the questioning phase of the presentation about the manpower implications of closing the administrative data centres at Marcon Chemicals.

In each extract the presenter handles a difficult question.

Complete the missing words in each of the presenter's answers.

Extract 1

Question

Excuse me, I would like to know how you have classified people as 'others' and 'high priority'. I mean, they all work for the same company, and many of them do very similar types of work. I'm not at all happy about it.

Answer

Yes, ... ,
.... , I .... we have to make decisions, and we do have to make judgements. And, there's another point, by reducing the number of data centres we're concentrating our strength and reducing costs.
.... the ....
of that.

Notice how the presenter shows he understands how the questioner feels, and then puts forward an alternative way of looking at the decision.

Extract 2

Question

How can you be sure of keeping someone who you've identified as high priority and also mobile? Aren't those the kind of people who could easily find work with one of our competitors?

Answer

Yes, ... a lot. .... the
company, ... , has an excellent record of
keeping staff. If .... look around, ... see .... how
many people have been with the company for more than five years.

Notice how the presenter acknowledges there is a problem, but then puts forward a very different way of looking at it.

Extract 3

Question

I've heard that Headquarters are also thinking of closing down the data centre at our plant in Trieste as well. Is that true?

Answer

.... , it's not for ....
.... You should ask John Roberts at the meeting on Friday.

Notice how the presenter evades this question by implying that he doesn't have enough responsibility to answer.

Extract 4

Question

Are the changes going to affect the staffing of the data centres at our plants?

Answer

I .... about manufacturing data centres at this stage. Could we .... later?

Notice how the presenter evades this question by delaying his answer until later.

Check your answers in the key C1

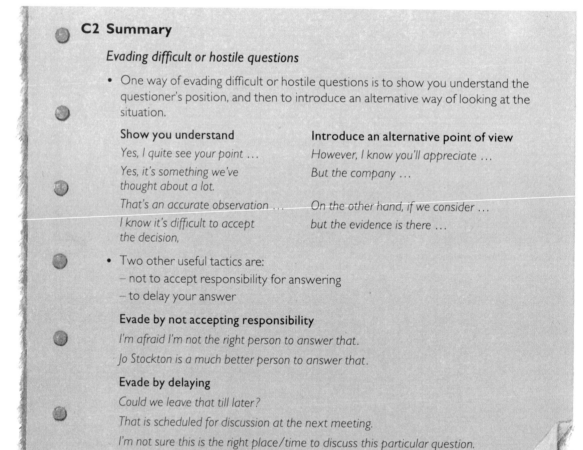

C2 Summary

Evading difficult or hostile questions

- One way of evading difficult or hostile questions is to show you understand the questioner's position, and then to introduce an alternative way of looking at the situation.

Show you understand	Introduce an alternative point of view
Yes, I quite see your point ...	*However, I know you'll appreciate ...*
Yes, it's something we've thought about a lot.	*But the company ...*
That's an accurate observation ...	*On the other hand, if we consider ...*
I know it's difficult to accept the decision,	*but the evidence is there ...*

- Two other useful tactics are:
  – not to accept responsibility for answering
  – to delay your answer

Evade by not accepting responsibility

I'm afraid I'm not the right person to answer that.

Jo Stockton is a much better person to answer that.

Evade by delaying

Could we leave that till later?

That is scheduled for discussion at the next meeting.

I'm not sure this is the right place/time to discuss this particular question.

C3 Tasks

1. Read the following evading replies and categorise them under the headings below.
Follow the example.

Introducing an alternative topic/position	Not accepting responsibility	Delaying
	a	

a. I'm afraid that's not my field, really. Perhaps Dr Fielding would be able to help.
b. We're hoping to talk about that at the meeting next week.
c. Actually, I don't have these figures on me. Could I speak to you later?
d. Yes, I think it is important, but perhaps even more important is the inflation rate.

Check your answers in the key

2. Listen to tape C3.2.
You will hear six questions. Give evading replies following the instructions below.
Make your response after each question.
You will then hear a model version.

Example

Question   Could you show us the breakdown of your advertising budget?

Your response   ....

Model version   **Actually, I don't have those figures with me, but I can get them to you by the end of the week.**

Questions	Instructions
a.	You don't have the figures and promise to get them to her by the end of the week.
b.	Agree that it's a long time to wait. Then give an alternative point of view – will give us longer to really study the market.
c.	You're not in a position to answer and he should ask the Personnel Department.
d.	You don't want to say anything at this stage. Say that it will be discussed at the next meeting in Chicago.
e.	You prefer to leave the point for now – you will deal with it later in the presentation.
f.	Acknowledge four per cent is not a big increase, introduce another point of view – bonus payments are still at a high level.

D How to handle information – Offering help to clarify information

When handling the questioning phase of a presentation, it may be necessary to clarify points from the presentation. At this stage it is often helpful to show slides and transparencies again.

D1 Focus

 Listen to tape D1.

You will hear another extract from the questioning phase of the presentation about the decision to close all the administrative data centres at Marcon Chemicals.

In this extract the questioner asks for clarification of a point. Notice how the presenter deals with the request.

Complete the missing words in the extract. Then read the notes on the right.

Extract	Notes
Question	
I'm afraid that I'm not at all clear what's going to happen to the two different categories you mentioned, the 'high priorities', and 'others'.	*Says she doesn't understand*
Could I see that slide again?	*Asks for help*
Answer	
.... , ... This is the chart we looked at earlier, but	*Agrees and brings back the slide, then offers additional help*
.... be .... if .... our current plans .... you two more charts.	

Check your answers in the key **D1**

D2 Summary

Offering help to clarify information

- When responding to requests from an audience you may need to:

Agree to a request

Q: *Could we see that slide again?*

A: *Yes, of course/Certainly. This is the diagram we looked at earlier ...*

Offer further help

This is the chart we looked at earlier, but perhaps it will be clearer if I show you two more charts.

Would you like to see another slide?

It might help if I spoke a little more about ...

I have another transparency which gives more details about ...

D3 Tasks

I. The visual below is one of the transparencies from the presentation about closing the administrative data centres. It shows the actions which are planned for the employees who have been identified as high priorities.

Study the information on the visual.

If you were an employee at Marcon what questions would you want to ask?

HIGH PRIORITIES
NEW CAREER DEVELOPMENT Inside or outside local area **Actions** Identify vacant positions Identify positions which will soon be vacant Stop recruitment Identify and plan necessary training

There is no key to this task.

📼 **2.** Listen to tape D3.2. You will now hear three questions from the audience, requesting help. You are the presenter. Reply to each request for help following the instructions below. Give your reply after each request.

You will then hear a model version.

Question	Instruction
a.	Agree – offer a document which you've prepared on the subject.
b.	Agree – explain you are having a meeting to discuss training implications. Invite the questioner to the meeting.
c.	Agree – offer to show a slide again. It shows how you've classified the 60 staff affected by the close-down of the data centres.

E Activities

1. Choose a visual you have used during a presentation. Then prepare questions and answers following the frameworks below.

Frameworks

A   **B**

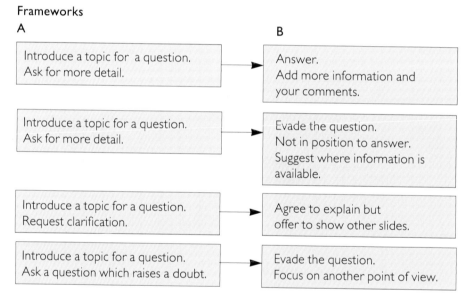

2. The questioning activity

Stage 1: Preparation

A You are attending an informal meeting, and you have been asked unexpectedly to give a brief presentation.

Your task is to prepare a quick presentation of one of the following:
– an unpopular decision
– the implications of a decision for your department or company

B You are the other participants at this meeting.

Your task is to think about the kind of questions you might want to ask in this type of situation. Check through the summaries in this unit.

Stage 2: The presentation

A Give your presentation.

B Listen to the presentation and take some notes about points you want to raise, other information you need, or points you need to clarify.

Stage 3: The questioning phase

A Invite questions from the audience. Be prepared to answer the questions, but evade any which you don't feel able, or willing to answer.

B Ask your questions. Remember to introduce the topic of the question before you actually ask it.

Answer key

A Preparation

A1
a. 1, 9
b. 3, 4, 6
c. 5, 7, 8, 2

A2 📼
1. How many data centres did you say will have to close?
2. I agree that sub-contracting is the best solution, but can you explain why people weren't informed about the decision straight away?
3. Isn't there a major security risk involved in sub-contracting to an outside supplier?
4. I can see big advantages in a single data centre, but is 1993 realistic?
5. You said some staff will be transferred to our manufacturing data centres. Does that mean a big expansion in their activity?
6. Isn't it the case that the decision to close down the data centres was taken months ago?
7. Could you give us some more information about how you propose to deal with retraining?
8. I have a question about the data centres. What will happen to them after they close down?
9. I'm not really clear about the timescale we'll be working to. Could you explain it again?

A2
a. 3, 4, 6
b. 1, 2, 5, 7, 8, 9

B What to say

B1 📼
Extract 1
QUESTIONER: Yes, I wonder if you could say a little more about the trend for Aqua-Sparkle. Is it seasonal, or is there another explanation for the fall-off in sales in the early part of the year?

PRESENTER: Well, it is seasonal to a certain extent. **Are you looking** at the January/February figures?

Extract 2
QUESTIONER: Excuse me, but when you mentioned the growth in profits, did you mean to say that the company is going to have more money to invest in plant and equipment next year?

PRESENTER: **So**, do we plan to plough back profits into investments for production next year? **For which product lines?**

Extract 3
QUESTIONER: Could I have another look at the slide which shows when we'll break even?

PRESENTER: **I'm sorry. I** didn't **hear**. Which slide was it?

B1
See tapescript B1 above. The missing words are in **bold**.

B3.1
a. ii b. i c. iii

B3.1 📼
a. QUESTIONER: We were rather concerned about the apparent intention to reduce numbers of staff in Brussels and Paris. Could you confirm the numbers in each place and what your intention is concerning their future?

PRESENTER: So, you'd like some information about the manpower implications for both sites.

b. QUESTIONER: Yes, my name is Dr Okamato and I would like to refer to your last slide. The reason is my colleagues in Sendai are working on a similar project and I would be interested in some detailed answers to some specific points.

PRESENTER: Excuse me Dr Okamato, but where is it you're from?

c. QUESTIONER: Many of my colleagues are concerned about the plans to license the product. Can you tell us something more about that?

PRESENTER: Excuse me, but which product are you referring to?

B3.2

a. Questioner — You talked about the sales figures for the first two quarters of the year and you mentioned that the trend was surprising. Could you comment on that further?

Your response ....

Model version **Sorry, but sales for which product line?**

b. Questioner — Yes. My name is Dr Maurice Brotherton. I have a question about field trials for Karate 3000E.

Your response ....

Model version **Excuse me. What was the product number?**

c. Questioner — As I understand it, your forecasts for agricultural products are quite optimistic. You mentioned fertilizers as being a real growth area. What do you think are the underlying reasons for this? Have we broken into new market areas?

Your response ....

Model version **So you'd like an explanation for our confidence in fertilizers as a major growth area in the coming years?**

d. Questioner — I'm not clear about how you want us to interpret the trend. You say that the first quarter saw a sharp fall, but when you spoke about the second quarter, which to my mind was equally disappointing, you seemed optimistic. Could you say something about that?

Your response ....

Model version **So, why am I so optimistic about the figures for the second quarter?**

C How to use tactics

C1

Extract 1

QUESTIONER: Excuse me, I would like to know how you have classified people as 'others' and 'high priority'. I mean, they all work for the same company, and many of them do very similar types of work. I'm not at all happy about it.

PRESENTER: Yes, **I quite see your point. However,** I **know you'll understand** we have to make decisions, and we do have to make judgements. And there's another point, by reducing the number of data centres we're concentrating our strength, and reducing costs. **I'm sure you can see** the **value** of that.

Extract 2

QUESTIONER: How can you be sure of keeping someone who you've identified as high priority and also mobile? Aren't those the kind of people who could easily find work with one of our competitors?

PRESENTER: Yes, **we've thought about that** a lot. **But** the company, **as you know**, has an excellent record of keeping staff. If **you** look around, **you'll** see **just** how many people have been with the company for more than five years.

Extract 3

QUESTIONER: I've heard that Headquarters are also thinking of closing down the data centre at our plant in Trieste as well. Is that true?

PRESENTER: **Actually**, it's not for **me to comment on that**. You should ask John Roberts at the meeting on Friday.

Extract 4

QUESTIONER: Are the changes going to affect the staffing of the data centres at our plants?

PRESENTER: I **don't think we should talk** about the manufacturing data centres at this stage. Could we **leave it until** later?

C1

See tapescript C1 above. The missing words are in **bold**.

C3.1

Introducing an alternative topic/position	d
Not accepting responsibility	a
Delaying	b c

C3.2 🔲

a. Question — Could you show us the breakdown of your advertising budget?

Your response ....

Model version — **Actually, I don't have the figures with me, but I can get them to you by the end of the week.**

b. Question — You said we won't be in a position to sign the contract till September. Doesn't that mean we'll lose out in the market?

Your response ....

Model version — **I agree it is a long time to wait. On the other hand, it will give us longer to really study the market.**

c. Question — You said that the office is overstaffed. Does this mean we'll have to stop all recruitment for next year?

Your response ....

Model version — **I'm afraid I'm not in a position to answer that question. You should ask the Personnel Department.**

d. Question — If control of marketing passes to Brussels, will that mean major restructuring of country sales teams?

Your response ....

Model version — **Actually, I don't want to say anything about that at this stage. We'll be discussing it at the next meeting in Chicago.**

e. Question — You mentioned some problems with our packaging suppliers. Could you tell us something more about that?

Your response ....

Model version — **I'd prefer to leave that point for now, as I'll be dealing with it specifically later in the presentation.**

f. Question — I'd like to ask a question about why pay agreements for this year are still in the region of four per cent. Could you comment on that?

Your response ....

Model version — **Yes, I agree four per cent isn't a very big increase. On the other hand, our bonus payments are still at a very high level.**

D How to handle information

D1 🔲

QUESTIONER: I'm afraid that I'm not at all clear what's going to happen to the two different categories you mentioned, the 'high priorities', and 'others'. Could I see that slide again?

PRESENTER: **Yes, of course.** This is the chart we looked at earlier, but **perhaps it will** be **clearer** if **I summarise** our current plans **by showing** you two more charts.

D1

See tapescript D1 above. The missing words are in **bold**.

D3.2 🔲

a. Question: — Excuse me, but in the slide you just showed us there is mention of new career development. Could you explain more about that?

Your response ....

Model version — **Yes, of course. But it might be more useful for you to have a look at a document which I have prepared on the subject.**

b. Question — Retraining is one of the options you mentioned on the last slide. Is there something more you can tell us about that?

Your response ....

Model version — **Certainly, but we're having a meeting to look at training implications tomorrow morning, would you like to come?**

c. Question — I'm still not clear how many people you're talking about as 'High Priorities'. Could you explain that again.

Your response ....

Model version — **Yes, of course, but perhaps it would help if we had another look at this slide, which shows how we've classified all 60 data staff.**